WHAT OTHERS ARE SAYING ABOUT LUCY'S BOOKS

VAGABOND HOLES '... a fast-paced, lively read that makes poetry and art enjoyable for even the most cynical yobbo' — Matt Coyte, *Rolling Stone*. '... crucial reading for anyone interested in Australia's music history' — Deborah Crabtree, *Bookseller + Publisher*. '... an epic work' — Julian Tompkin, *Sunset Magazine*. '... moving ... funny ... heartfelt' — Iain Shedden, *The Australian*. '... a compelling read' — Ray Purvis, *The West Australian*. '... a little gem ... entertaining, essential ... I will return to this book often' — *Triffids.com*. **THE WAR ON DEMOCRACY** '... I found myself unable to put the book down ... lively, sardonic and very entertaining' — Kitty van Vuuren, *Media International Australia*. '... crying out to be written' — Georgina Murray, *Overland*. '... compelling ... provocative ... so timely' — Mark Howie, *English in Australia*. '... postmodernists have become the red-headed stepchild of academe' — Cassandra Wilkinson, *Australian Literary Review*. '... entertaining if sometimes bizarre' — Mark Bennister, *Reviews in Australian Studies*. '... blood sport' — Luke Slattery, *On Line Opinion*. '... unusually vicious polemic' — Christopher Pearson, *The Australian*. '... insightful ... often hilarious' — Brian Michael Musgrove, *M/C Journal*. 'Lucy ... remains a kind of parish priest in the much-diminished postmodern church' — Luke Slattery, *The Australian*. 'It is precisely this way of imagining democracy that has facilitated ... so many of the rights now enjoyed by citizens' — Adam Gall, *Thinking Culture*. '... provocative and entertaining. Don't miss it' — *The Age*. 'The authors score many palpable hits ...' — Rodney Tiffen, *Australian Book Review*. 'Textual sex!!!' — *Keepleft.org*. '... a most timely book' — Norman Abjorensen, *The Canberra Times*. **A DERRIDA DICTIONARY** 'A saucy, sparkling success' — John D. Caputo, Villanova University. '... ironic, iconoclastic and earthy' — Stuart

Hannabuss, *Reference Reviews* (US). '... ranges with considerable intellectual flair from Hegel to Geri Halliwell, fascism to Francis Fukuyama, the philosophy of consciousness to celebrity' — Anthony Elliott, *The Times Literary Supplement*. 'It is the kind of book whose wit makes one want to read excerpts to colleagues, and it is precisely this lightness of tone that makes Lucy's book so pedagogically useful ... Highly recommended' — S. Barnett, *Choice* (US). 'There is sharpness, wit and high seriousness in every entry' — Peggy Kamuf, University of Southern California. **BEYOND SEMIOTICS** '... full of surprises' — Scott Simpkins, *The Semiotic Review of Books*. '... eloquent' — Darren Tofts, *Rhizomes*. **POSTMODERN LITERARY THEORY: AN ANTHOLOGY** '... essential' — Alistair Paterson, *Stylus Poetry Journal*. **POSTMODERN LITERARY THEORY: AN INTRODUCTION** '... difficult but rewarding' — Peter Holbrook, *Quadrant*. '... magnificent' — McKenzie Wark, *The Australian Higher Education Supplement*. '... learned ... suggestive ... inspired' — K. Toloyan, *Choice* (US). '... very useful introduction' — Sabine Buchholz, *At the Edge of Art and Insanity*. '... a critical account of the difference between postmodernism and poststructuralism' — Claire Colebrook, *Sub-stance*. 'As Niall Lucy reminds us, Derrida has never quite given up on the signified ...' — Horst Ruthrof, *New Literary History*. '... enlightening' — Elizabeth H. Jones, *Spaces of Belonging*. '... perceptive' — Keith Jenkins, *Why History?* **DEBATING DERRIDA** '... lucid and pedagogical' — Juliana De Nooy, *Derrida, Kristeva and the Dividing Line*. '... a fabulous little book' — Robert Briggs, *Roughtheory. org*. '... clear and very readable, and never falls into the trap of oversimplification' — Tony Thwaites, University of Queensland.

POMO OZ

FEAR AND LOATHING DOWNUNDER

NIALL LUCY

FREMANTLE PRESS
fine independent publishing

TITLES BY NIALL LUCY

The Ballad of Moondyne Joe (Fremantle Press, 2011/forthcoming), with John Kinsella

Activist Poetics: Anarchy in the Avon Valley by John Kinsella (2010), editor

Vagabond Holes: David McComb & The Triffids (Fremantle Press, 2009), co-edited with Chris Coughran

Beautiful Waste: Poems by David McComb (Fremantle Press, 2009), co-edited with Chris Coughran

Plagiarism! (From Work to Détournement), special issue of *Angelaki: Journal of Theoretical Humanities* (2009), co-edited with John Kinsella

The War on Democracy: Conservative Opinion in the Australian Press (2006), with Steve Mickler

A Derrida Dictionary (2004)*

Beyond Semiotics: Text, Culture and Technology (2001)*

Postmodern Literary Theory: An Anthology (2000), editor

Philosophy and Cultural Studies, special issue of *Continuum: Journal of Media and Culture* (1998), editor

Postmodern Literary Theory: An Introduction (1997)*

Debating Derrida (1995)

*Translations (extant and forthcoming) in Arabic, German, Japanese, Portuguese, Serbian and Turkish

For Sam, without mercy

CONTENTS

PREFACE

Feeling pissed off at the humbug that was spouted by sanctimonious politicians and other authorities when *The Chaser* cracked the best joke of 2007 (the fake motorcade at the APEC summit), I ended up writing this book. I didn't quite know it was going to turn out that way at the time, as I explain in the Introduction, but in retrospect that's how it all began. I refer to *The Chaser* episode at the beginning of the second section, 'Running On/BORDER LINES', but my distaste for sanctimony runs all the way through the book (and not for the first time), as it does, I think, throughout postmodernism. So to the extent that this is a book defending pomo from pious attacks downunder, it's also about how much I hate po-faced piety.

I am grateful to those who helped me along the way: Peta Bowden, Rob Briggs, Marion May Campbell, Claire Colebrook, Chris Coughran, John Frow, Bill Green, Lisa Gye, Mark Howie, John Kinsella, Steve Mickler, Jane Mummery, Sam Stevenson, Darren Tofts and Ken Wark. I am especially grateful to Georgia Richter, my editor at Fremantle Press, for all her support as well as her astute comments. I am also grateful to the editors and anonymous referees of the journals in which earlier versions of the chapters appeared: Chapter 2 in *Changing English* (2008), Chapter 3 in *Transformations* (2008) and Chapter 4 in *English in Australia* (2009). I presented an earlier version of Chapter 1 at the 'Derrida Today' conference in Sydney (2008), and I thank the organisers, Nicole Anderson and Nick Mansfield, for the invitation to do so. An earlier version of 'Running On/BORDER LINES' was published in *Derrida Today* (2008), and I thank the editors for the opportunity to appear in that journal. An even earlier version appeared as 'Poetry and Deconstruction' in *Language Systems: After Prague Structuralism*, edited by Louis Armand (2007), based on a paper I gave at the structuralism conference at Charles University, Prague, that year; my thanks to Louis Armand and Martin Prochazka, the organisers of the conference, for inviting me to present.

INTRODUCTION

'There is nothing outside of the text,' Jacques Derrida wrote in 1967, and civilisation as we know it began to fall apart at the seams. Then, in 2001, some of Derrida's readers blew up the World Trade Center in New York ... in the name of deconstruction. Then some more of his readers conspired to wreak havoc on Wall Street in 2008 for the purpose of deconstructing capitalism by manufacturing the GEC.

Such is the devastation caused by Derrida's ideas — the deaths, the ruined lives, the previously unimagined scale of worldwide social and economic chaos — it's a wonder anyone is left to read this book. Not since Marx has one man's name aroused such fear and loathing, nor since communism has there been a movement so insidious as deconstruction.

Preposterous as this little narrative may seem, it's a story that in one form or another is retold on more or less a daily basis in Oz. Derrida may not always be inscribed directly, but if only by inference he's always embedded in it as one of the alleged architects of something called 'postmodernism' that's supposed to be responsible for real-world catastrophic effects on Western culture. Precisely because the story *is* utterly preposterous, of course, it has to be repeated often in the hope of standing in for common sense among those — the vast majority of my fellow citizens — who otherwise couldn't give a flying fuck about Derrida or deconstruction, and why should they? Why should 'Derrida,' any more than 'Shakespeare' — or 'Elvis' — command unbridled fidelity, when there are people dying out there? When the real world outside the text is riven with injustices and violence? Why, to take but two pressing examples, should 'Derrida' matter when ordinary Australians are faced with declining living standards due to 'fluctuations' in an economy they neither own nor influence significantly, or when the health rates and life expectancy of white Australians currently far exceed — for no acceptable reason — those of black Australians?

This book is my attempt to answer these questions, at least for myself. The essays in it were written across the space of a year or so, beginning (with 'Running On/BORDER LINES', the second part of the book) in the latter half of 2007. At the same time as I was writing that piece I was working on a couple of other essays, each of them commissioned separately, and somewhere in the midst of this (say, around January or February 2008) I realised, without realising, that I was writing 'a book': a book about the consequences of arguing that there's nothing outside the text. Books come from many possible sources, in other words, and only sometimes from what might be called a writer's conscious intent, which tells us something about 'writing.'

When we write something, we can never quite get outside of 'writing,' the history or economy of writing, let's say, to a place from which we could exercise total control over what we write (and especially not over how it might be read). We might occasionally coin a neologism or use a punctuation mark or a generic device eccentrically, but by and large we're constrained to write within conventions that precede us. These conventions don't 'imprison' us, however, since clearly they enable all kinds of writing — creative, critical, scientific, imaginative and so on — to get done. Once in a blue moon a book comes along — *Tristram Shandy, Finnegans Wake* — or a 'new' mode of writing appears (prose in the eighteenth century, free verse in the twentieth) that might be said both to break with conventions and to expand or realign them, but most of the time we don't have any kind of individual power to influence what 'writing' means when we write something. This is true of 'writers,' too. Whoever wins the Miles Franklin next year will be most unlikely to have written a book that could change the meaning of 'writing,' and so the award will go — and there could be nothing wrong with this — to the text that is seen to best reproduce an idea of 'literature' that precedes it, an idea it may be said to contribute to or participate in but which did not originate with it. On the model of this example, what could be so dangerously radical or scandalous about arguing that there is nothing outside the text except more text: in this case, more writing? Here, on the contrary, all we'd be saying would be something perfectly banal: that writers never get outside 'writing' — the history of writing as a discontinuous or ever-changing 'system' of values and conventions — when they write. None of us does.

Usually, though, when this claim is cited disapprovingly as 'self-evident' nonsense, it's taken to mean that there is no such thing as truth, which in turn is meant to be a very silly thing to think or say even though it's supposed to be the core belief of many if not most humanities academics and secondary-school English teachers, among others, in Australia today. For my own part, I've never met or read anyone who thinks there's no such thing as truth. But even if some people did believe this, I don't — on the contrary — see how they could draw their warrant for believing it from reading Derrida or anything associated with deconstruction or, more broadly, postmodernism.

Why, then, is 'postmodernism' so often accused of representing the belief that there is no such thing as truth, when no one who could conceivably be described as a postmodernist has ever said this? There are several possible answers to such a question, some of which I broach here. In Chapter 1, for instance, I argue that Miranda Devine accuses 'postmodern' art of being paedophilic in the complete ex-nomination of a decidedly 'unpostmodern' — indeed pre-modern — institution, the Catholic Church, the history of whose systemic abuse of minors has only recently begun to come to light. Here, where the occasion refers to the public scandal in 2008 surrounding the exhibition of Bill Henson's photographs of naked children, the inference is that it follows from believing that because there's no such thing as truth, there could be no such thing as an inappropriate image. Henson's photography is able to count as 'art,' in other words, due only to the amoral latitude afforded by postmodernism, an unhappy confluence that Devine feels is deserving of her umbrage. Meanwhile ... psst ... what about the priests?

In Chapter 2, I turn to another recent scandal involving 'postmodernism,' one that remains ongoing: the far from universally civil debate surrounding the teaching of critical literacy ('postmodern English') in Australian high schools today. The occasion here has to do with the perhaps unlikely intervention of eminent cultural studies scholar Graeme Turner, whose adverse approach to critical literacy is not entirely inconsistent with popular media forms of demonising 'progressive' — or, as I prefer, democratic — attitudes to education. While certainly I don't think Turner shares the interests of conservative opponents of 'postmodernism,' this is not to say that on the present occasion at least he doesn't share certain assumptions with them. And just as expressions of moral outrage over the alleged paedophilic effects of 'postmodern' art distract from the injustices of inherent paedophilia in the churches, so does the condemnation of 'postmodern' education obscure the need for public schools to receive better resources and public teachers better pay. Want to fix problems in public education? Stop putting public money into private schools and give it back to the public sector, and — faster than you can say 'Kevin Donnelly' or 'education crisis' — watch the attrition from public to private schools ... vanish.

If there is a 'crisis' in education, which is taken routinely to refer to the public sector pretty much exclusively, who could really believe that 'postmodernism' and not state treasury is responsible for it? But Kevin Donnelly (the publication of whose *Dumbing Down* is the occasion for Chapter 3, co-written with Steve Mickler) insists that 'postmodernism,' as a pedagogy, a set of ideas, has ... well, dumbed down Gen Y as it will the iGen. In order to argue this, he (and others too of course) must first misattribute to postmodernism all manner of ludicrous ideas and beliefs such that any reader who accepted them would be left with no choice but to condemn 'postmodernism' for 'its' intellectual shortcomings and twisted, 'anti-Western' agenda. By now, then, it's possible to identify the moves that must be made in order to construct postmodernism as an affront to common sense and decency that, in its disrespect for plain language and timeless values, puts our very way of life at risk. I discuss these moves in Chapter 4, occasioned this time by the publication of Gavin Kitching's *The Trouble with Theory*, a book that received a good deal of favourable press coverage on release in 2008. Exemplary in its criticism of an object that it never engages with, Kitching's book shows that the key move in such a reading of 'postmodernism' makes it imperative *not* to read.

Perhaps I should mention at this point that I have no particular allegiance to the term 'postmodernism,' and I don't think of myself as a 'postmodernist.' I don't reject these labels, but I don't, as they say, 'identify' strongly with them either, except to defend them from ignorance. What I'm trying to show in these four chapters (the first part of the book) is that what others deride as 'postmodernism' — and for all I care they could call it 'orange marmalade' — describes in fact a genuinely speculative and critical approach to ideas, and to creative modes of textual production, which I think is the real source of contention here. It's that approach — one I associate with the Enlightenment — to which I do feel a very strong sense of allegiance; and so for me 'postmodernism' is to be defended in so far as it can be seen as a continuation of the Enlightenment by other means.

The problem for those who oppose postmodernism, as I see it, isn't 'postmodernism' as such; the problem is that there's too much questioning of authority going on nowadays, especially among young people, which is troublesome for the powerful interests that authorities — governments, businesses, the churches, the media and so on — represent. 'Postmodernism' is only ever condemned in order to protect the interests of a particular authority or even the general concept of authority. So Devine blames paedophilia on 'postmodernism,' thinking to protect the authority of the priesthood; Turner scorns it, in the guise of secondary-school 'critical literacy,' for threatening the authority of university cultural studies; Donnelly attacks it in defence of the authority of 'the West'; and Kitching ridicules it for questioning the authority of male elders. In every case, a strong or established set of interests prevails over those pertaining to a weaker or more emergent set.

This isn't to say I think that all those who are critical of 'postmodernism' are consciously on the side of power and privilege. What interests me, however, are not their personal motives, but what their ideas and positions commit us to engage with. I simply don't, for instance, buy the line — regardless of the motives of whoever's peddling it — that too much theory and not enough literature (too much Derrida and not enough Shakespeare) is to blame for the creation of a moral vacuum in the West that terrorists are using to their advantage! Whenever 'postmodernism' is accused of wielding undue 'influence,' indeed, I can't help but wonder what 'postmodernists' are using to fund it. We all know where the funds came from to finance the GEC, but surely no one could believe that humanities academics or high-school English teachers command the sort of economic, social or political power to create an event on a comparable scale.

All of this is not outside the accusation that 'postmodernism' represents the belief that there is no such thing as truth. In the first part of the book, therefore, I try to show that this accusation, whenever it is made, always harbours particular interests, and interests are never outside of texts (try locating, for example, as a pre-textual, a-contextual, utterly unmediated, uncontested fact, the interests of a multinational corporation, say, or those of a disadvantaged social group). So this first part is a defence of postmodernism against a series of egregious attacks that, for me, serve less-than-democratic interests. As an idea and an ideal, the concept of democracy (as Derrida argues in *Specters of Marx*) holds open the promise of a better future to come; and, just as the future can never be made actual, democracy, too, must always remain to come.[1] In so far as attacks on 'postmodernism' are not responsive to that promise, then, I don't think they're democratic.

If these first four chapters are characterised by a rhetorically combative tone, I hope it will be conceded that I didn't start the fight. I chose simply not to walk away from it. I did so not because I don't believe there's such a thing as truth, but precisely because I do believe it; I just don't believe in 'the' truth as such. I don't believe, for example, that the truth of our current economic situation compels ordinary Australians to exercise wage restraint in the national interest. On the contrary, I believe it is true that wage restraints are in the interests of the corporate sector. I believe that 'the' truth, in a word, is always on the side of power and privilege, and I prefer to side elsewhere.

In the second part of the book — 'Running On/BORDER LINES' — I turn to an affirmation of the ideas I defend in the first part, with a view to showing that power and privilege are always vested in the uncritical acceptance of authority. Since deconstruction always puts authority — and authorities — into question, it's easy to see why Derrida's ideas continue to be a problem for those who would rather things stayed just the way they are. But if this were only what a 'theorist' (someone who doesn't value or appreciate the great works of Western culture) could say, it must surely seem incongruous that this section was occasioned by an invitation from the poet John Kinsella to write the introduction to his *Derrida Poems*, a tribute to his friendship with Derrida. Clearly (albeit, according to myths about 'postmodernism,' no less surprisingly also), Kinsella has no difficulty in reconciling a love of poetry with an interest in Derrida's work, even though poets are supposed to regard 'theory' as anathema.

That piece slowly grew, across several months and places, into something larger than an introduction to John's book, a book that, for reasons best known to him, he wants to appear in French before it appears in English. (I understand that it's being translated into French for publication in a year or so.) While I started out with an interest in redressing accusations against Kinsella's work, usually of the ad hominem variety, I soon became interested in thinking about possible relations between poetry and deconstruction, since these terms are often couched as opposites by those who see 'postmodernism' as 'anti-literary,' and indeed an early version of the then unfinished essay (which I gave at a conference on structuralism at Charles University, Prague, in October 2007) was published under the title of 'Poetry and Deconstruction'. Above all, though, I developed an interest in what a friendship between an Australian poet and a 'French' philosopher, both of them controversial figures, had to say more generally about Australia's supplementary relations to Europe, which I chose to mark rhetorically (in imitation of Derrida) through the inclusion of an extended supplement in the form of a 'footnote' that isn't quite a footnote. You'll see. Among other possible effects, the device is meant to mirror Australia's place downunder, below or at the foot of European concepts of culture and history, and at the same time to show that the supplement is not outside the text — of the essay, or an idea of Europe as central to the meaning of such concepts. Australia's 'difference' derives, that is to say, from the powerful concepts of culture and history, together with the concept of nature, having been defined in advance in European terms, but that difference is also necessary to the authority of those definitions. Cast in the role of a supplement, 'Australia' is at the margins of a centre that is European through and through.

But what if centre–margin relations (not only between Europe and Australia, but also, for example, between 'truth' and 'postmodernism') were not naturally occurring phenomena, but in a sense always the result of political and ethical decisions? What might be the consequences of this for, say ... I don't know, ordinary Australians and disadvantaged social groups?

That's all I'm asking here.

1. TABLOID DECONSTRUCTION

Whenever I see the word *breasts* I get a hard on. Call me old-fashioned, though, but the word *crotch* has never done it for me. I've never been remotely interested in a woman's 'crotch,' the place where her body forks, from the Old French for 'pitchfork.' I'm a 'cunt' man myself, a word of disputed origins that may or may not have its root (badda badda boom!) in an Old Norse word no one seems to know the meaning of. The first recorded instance of it in English is the thirteenth-century London street name, *Gropecuntlane*, where no doubt a good strumpet could be had for a groat or two. But regardless of where it comes from, for me it has to be 'cunt' every time.

So when I read Miranda Devine's description in the *Sydney Morning Herald* for 22 May 2008 of the invitation to that night's opening of the Bill Henson exhibition at the Roslyn Oxley9 Gallery in Paddington, first I got turned on and then very quickly turned off:

> The invitation to the exhibition features a large photo of a girl, the light shining on her hair, eyes downcast, dark shadows on her sombre, beautiful

> face, and the budding breasts of puberty on full
> display, her hand casually covering her crotch.
> (Devine 2008a)[1]

In a word, Devine's 'crotch' leaves me singularly unaroused. Why didn't she just say 'cunt' instead?

The simple answer to this seeming conundrum is that Devine wasn't trying to arouse me sexually, but on the contrary to arouse my moral indignation over what she sees as the exploitative, indeed the mundanely exploitative, sexualisation of children in the media today. She was not writing as an eroticist, then; much less as a pornographer. She was writing as a journalist.

So what kind of writer is a journalist? In a sense a journalist is not really a 'writer' at all, which is what got Tom Wolfe and that crowd into so much trouble (see Lucy 2006). Understood as journalism, writing assumes the status of photography. This is why reading an old newspaper is like communing with the dead, in the knowledge (or rather the phantasmagoric apprehension) that all this *once was*. As time recedes, this haunting effect intensifies: the older the news story is, the more aware we are that those whose names appear in it are gone forever. They are not just dead, but *irreversibly* dead. Each once was and is no more. Like reading names off gravestones in a cemetery, reading an old newspaper article puts us in some kind of spooky contact with those who once lived but are no longer living, and who will never live again.

This hallucination, whether felt intensely or apprehended vaguely on reading news stories from the past, is the basis of the journalistic reality effect. A modern-day (or postmodern) journalist doesn't so much write as point a keyboard at the world, capturing what 'was' or still 'is.' For this effect to come off it has to be believed that between text and outside-text, or between what Roland Barthes calls the spectrum or image-object and the noeme (see Barthes 1982), there is perfect continuity. And for this to happen, for this hallucinatory correspondence to appear inviolable, above all what has to be effaced is the *grain* of the reporting. This is why Devine says 'crotch,' because all females (and indeed all males) harbour a place where the body forks. But only a woman has a 'cunt,' and then only in certain contexts. The word 'crotch,' then, is less a word than a linguistic photo of its referent, an analogic, a-contextual trace of something that just indubitably 'is' outside of language. But the word 'cunt' is digital. To use it, except for pointedly poetic or pornographic purposes, or between sexually consenting adults, is to risk not only liberal censure for causing offence but also legal censure for being 'obscene.' Such a risk — of errancy, of misinterpretation — is a condition of the digital, for which the relationship between text and outside-text is of the order of the *dis*continuous.

Instead of giving rise to the spontaneous belief that *this was*, the discontinuity of the digital causes us to wonder whether, as Bernard Stiegler puts it, '*perhaps* this was not' (Stiegler 2002, 157). Perhaps this was not a 'cunt,' but only a feminine 'crotch' — the place where a female body forks. Such doubt is intrinsic to writing, as we know from Plato, but — as we know from Derrida — it cannot be opposed to the self-presence or seeming immediacy of speech but only to the *belief* that speech is a guarantee of presence.[2] In this way the distinction Stiegler draws between the analogic photo and the digital 'photographic' image (or what he calls the analogico-digital image, since it is not quite a photograph at all) is a form, a postmodern uptake, as it were, of the speech–writing opposition.

Small wonder, then, that journalistic writing should try to pass off the phonological as the photological, which applies even to the writing of a 'soft' journalist, an opinion columnist, like Devine. No less than a philosopher or a 'hard' news reporter, an opinion columnist cannot afford to trade in opinions, since the reality effect (the realism) of journalistic writing depends on being seen as the other of the solipsistic and the perspectival. If to be a news reporter is to 'photograph' the actual in words, then an opinion columnist is a photographer of the esoteric — of public opinions and social moods. Each is an illusionist, of course, whose consummate professional trick is to efface the textuality of the written. What enables the trick to be pulled off, a trick journalism borrows from photography, which borrows it from speech, has to do with the *immediacy* of a textual appearance that therefore goes unnoticed as text, as if, like speech and photography, journalism offered direct and 'unmediated' access to the real.[3]

Take the analogic photo, which is produced when light from an object is captured through a camera lens before being imprinted on photographic paper. What distinguishes the moment of capture is that it is immediate: *this was* and here, now, *it is*. What part of this process is 'textual'? The photons reflected or emitted by *that* object, having been trapped in a solution of silver halide chemicals, are now here on *this* piece of paper. Where's the mediation in this, for surely the immediacy by which the transfer of light occurs describes a perfect continuity between the object and the photograph of that object? How, then, could a photograph be a 'text'?

This is precisely the question Devine asks in a follow-up to her Henson piece in response to those seeking to legitimise Henson's photographs of naked juveniles by locating them within a tradition of European art. To compare Henson to the grand masters is to 'miss the point that Henson's art is photography,' Devine argues, 'which has none of the ambiguity of painting' (Devine 2008b). By appealing to the 'this was-ness' of a photograph, Devine thinks to efface its textuality. For her, then, photographic indubitability must be assumed to be total when in fact it is only ever partial, confined not to the 'photographic' as such but to the photo-chemical. Yes, there is a photo-chemical continuity between a Henson photo of a naked minor and the real-life model of the photo, but everything else about the photograph is discontinuous and therefore open to interpretation. This is why it is possible to believe that photographs have been taken of UFOs and ghosts. In such cases the indubitability that *this* was, is less important than the question: *what* was?

Every photo is a photo of such-and-such an object, but this fact alone does not ground the meaning of a photograph or close it off from 'ambiguity.' Photographs are distinguished from paintings not by being less ambiguous or less interpretable, but for seeming to be less manipulable. While the subject of a painting may be anything, the spectrum of a photograph — what Stiegler calls the image-object that appears on photosensitive paper — is to a certain extent continuous with the real. Some form of essential correspondence links the photographic text to an outside that in some essential way determines that text. But of course the analogic image-object is never fully determined — photographically or textually — by virtue of its photo-chemical relations to an outside. In a sense, then, such relations are no more textually determining than the mental-object of a surrealist painting, which is not to say that Dali's liquid clocks have the same ontological status as a photograph of the Twin Towers burning down. It is to say, though, that such a photograph cannot quite be an image *of* '9/11,' since the meaning of '9/11' cannot be allowed to be determined photo-chemically. So while indeed there are image-objects of things in the world, these are not transcendental signifieds.

Take the example of the so-called 'children overboard' affair, a case well known to Australians. On 10 October 2001, at the start of a federal election campaign, the Howard government sought to engender a vote-winning 'this was' effect by distributing carefully cropped photographs to the Australian media purporting to show Iraqi asylum seekers on board a wooden refugee boat from Indonesia, *The Olong*, throwing their children into the Indian Ocean about a hundred nautical miles north of Christmas Island a few days before, with the intention of blackmailing the nearby HMAS *Adelaide* into escorting them to Australia. Without pausing to question *what* 'was,' the media published the photos and straight away the Howard government, without any opposition from federal Labor, won public approval for its 'strong' decision not to grant refugee status to others who so clearly did not treat their children like us. But what the cropped photographs failed to show was that *The Olong* was sinking at the time. The asylum seekers in the water (only some of whom were children in any case) had not been thrown in, but had fallen in or jumped; this was the finding of a senate inquiry almost twelve months after the Howard government was re-elected with an increased majority on 11 November that year.

The 'children overboard' photographs showed, to be sure, that *something* was, but *what* it was turned out to be other than it seemed. Even when they were accepted as image-objects of children who had been thrown overboard by their parents, however, the photographs did not show that HMAS *Adelaide* had fired several warning shots across *The Olong* shortly before the photographs were taken. Hence they did not show that the people in the water — far from being alien to us — were indeed like us, since they were understandably frightened for their safety in what were undeniably dangerous circumstances. Everything 'outside' the photos or belonging to the context of their distribution to the media had to be suppressed in order to produce them as image-objects with a single, irrefutable referent: children overboard! Such a context included the electoral interests of the Howard government that were served by appealing to national anxieties surrounding the 'war on terror,' which made it seem imperative that every so-called asylum seeker should be treated as a potential suicide bomber. The irony, too, that most of the refugees on board *The Olong* were in fact victims of the 'war on terror' had to be suppressed, as did the fact that in the weeks following the release of the photos to the media, and as the election date drew closer, the Prime Minister's office instructed the Canberra Command Centre to withhold information on *The Olong* refugees which might allow the media to 'humanise' them.[4]

As it happens, the initial truth status of the 'children overboard' photographs turned out to rely on a 'this was' effect that … wasn't. But it is neither here nor there that the image-objects of the photos are understood now to be of a different order than before; nor is it of much significance that those 'image-objects' are not strictly image-objects at all, but simulacra, since in fact the 'children overboard' pictures were taken with a digital camera. While there is a difference between the analogic image-object and the digital spectrum, the latter being always 'something *other than* the photonic ectoplasm of a *this was*' (Stiegler 2002, 153), the difference is not that of a naive distinction between the actual and the virtual. Otherwise, for this distinction to hold, it would have to be believed that only the photographs submitted to the media should count as actual evidence in the 'children overboard' affair, everything else being virtual, speculative, subjective, supplementary. It would be as if the *text* of the affair should be situated in the absence of any context, replete with a meaning that was never actively produced — sorted, sifted and hierarchicised against a background of national fears and national interests — but innately given.

Such a distinction — between the actual and the virtual, text and outside-text, essence and supplement — continues to draw its force from the refusal of what might be called deconstruction's baseline claim: that 'there is nothing outside of the text' (Derrida 1976, 158). There is nothing outside of a context, that is to say, which is not to say that contexts are discrete and stable in themselves. But far from being obscurantist or silly, as this is often dismissed to be, the unextraordinary mundanity of deconstruction's insistence on the necessarily indeterminate nature of relations between text and outside-text could scarcely be better illustrated than in the 'children overboard' affair. If what is meant by a 'text' could be determined by its separation from everything alleged to be 'external' to or 'outside' of it, then in the present case the only allowable meanings of *The Olong* photos would be either 'children overboard' or '*not* children overboard.' Understood as a discrete entity of the order of the actual, like (say) a tile or a brick, a text can be thought to have a meaning that assumes the status of a 'this was' or a simulated 'this was' *effect*, which is to say it can be thought to have something like the equivalent of an actual referent. But textual meanings are never independent of contexts, so that textual referents are not pre-given but produced. The referent or simulated 'this was' *effect* of the 'children overboard' photographs was actively produced initially by appearing to separate the photographs from a context, or by contextualising them in the midst of a xenophobic fear of the other's predisposition to terrorism, and thereafter by contextualising them in respect of the Howard government's electoral interests. Hence the *text* of the affair is not reducible to something as seemingly determined as a referent ('children overboard' or '*not* children overboard'), since it includes at least the political interests of the Howard government; the readiness of the Labor Party, the media and the public to accept the photographs initially as confirmation of the potentially violent otherness of Asian and Middle Eastern people; and the fact that there were no consequences for Howard and his ministers when the senate inquiry found that the government had known for some time prior to the 2001 election (for at least several days if not weeks) that there was no evidence to justify the claim that refugees on *The Olong* had ever thrown their children overboard. Despite being advised by senior public servants and navy personnel, however, that the asylum seekers had *not* tossed their children into the open sea, the government failed to pass on this information to the media and the public. The 2001 re-election of the Howard government, then, was won, if only in part, on the back of a monstrously undemocratic deception. *So* undemocratic was it that, when it became known a year later that the government had deceived voters the year before, the street leading up to Parliament House in Canberra should have been re-named (to invoke another meaning of the 'c' word) *Gropecuntlane*. But of course that would have been obscene.

In such a context, whose limits have by no means been reached, why the coyness over a word? Ah yes, I remember now: because of its improper 'sexual' overtones when used or mentioned in reference to a child, and more generally because of its improper 'social' overtones when used or mentioned on inappropriate (or infelicitous) occasions. Such liberal niceties, however, delude us into thinking that texts are reducible to 'this was'-like referents or essential meanings and uses, so that an image-object of a naked child must be an image-object of a real-life naked child that was; and therefore it must be exploitatively arousing. Certainly it is true that the image-object of the invitation to the Henson exhibition that Devine refers to in her piece for 22 May 2008 actually *was* a real-life naked girl. But no less than the photographs in the 'children overboard' affair, this image-object cannot be said *to mean* simply in and of 'itself,' in the absence of a context. While it is more or less tautologically true that *this* photo of a naked child is a photo of *that* naked child, it is not otherwise true necessarily that the photo is abusive, exploitative, improper or obscene. It may be, but it does not *have* to be, any of these things. Indeed, Devine herself must know that textual meanings are never independent of contexts, since in the second instalment of her series of attacks on Henson's art she strays so far from the text at hand as to link Henson's photography to actual, real-life child sexual abuse in remote Aboriginal communities, only to go even further afield by making the extraordinarily offensive claim that Aboriginal mothers don't love their children as we love ours. In outback Indigenous communities, Devine says, 'the social norms we ['we' in the cities, or 'we' whites?] take for granted, *such as the love of a mother for her child*, have collapsed' (Devine 2008b, emphasis added)! What, like the 'love' of the dark-skinned asylum seekers on *The Olong* for their dark-skinned kids?

In the context of the arrival in Sydney in a few days — Devine's Sydney — of Joe Ratzinger (aka Pope Benedict XVI, who was either forced or chose to enlist in the Hitler Youth movement and thereafter the German army in World War II, depending on which version you believe), it is difficult to imagine why anyone claiming to want to protect children's sexual innocence would want to protest the exhibition of image-objects of naked minors at a private art gallery for the contemplation of, at best, a few hundred well-heeled patrons.[5] Statistics from around the world tell us that it is not photographers, artists, writers, philosophers or 'postmodernists' who, as a group, pose a sexual threat to minors. It is the priests and other clergy from the orthodox churches (albeit not exclusively) who pose such a threat. Children's actual sexual innocence is endangered not by the virtual paedophilia of art-house photography (nor indeed by the so-called 'corporate paedophilia' of the advertising world), but by the priests, who preach universal love and goodwill to all from the pulpit. It is the priest, pre-modern, seemingly liberal subject of a medieval, defiantly undeconstructed, undemocratic institution — an institution symbolically presided over by Ratzinger's Holy See — who threatens the very rights of children that Devine claims to want to defend. It is the priests, nuns and other clergy, after all, of the Vatican's emblematic dominion who have helped to produce the conditions of outback Indigenous communities in Australia today; and if Devine's moral indignation on behalf of a child's right to sexual probity were fair dinkum, her accusative finger would be directed not at Bill Henson, but at Pope Benedict XVI — or even her own town's Cardinal Pell — as a leader not of God's will on earth, but of the earth's leading paedophile ring. If Devine were fair dinkum, she'd want to say … *cunt!*

2. EVERYBODY LOVES RAYMOND WILLIAMS: CRITICAL LITERACY, CULTURAL STUDIES AND THE NEW INTERNATIONAL

I

The standard complaint against literary theory at university used to be that it destroys the pleasure of reading. So often was this said, that it feels now like some of us must have been spending more time defending theory than just doing it. But since 'theory' is no longer a scandalous topic at university, certainly not in the humanities, I began to think of late that everyone must finally be agreed that the theory-versus-pleasure brouhaha had always been a whopping furphy. I was wrong. On reading Graeme Turner's recent criticisms of contemporary secondary-school English studies in Australia, in an essay for the *International Journal of Cultural Studies* (Turner 2007), I see now that complaining about how theory destroys pleasure has not gone away. It has simply gone off campus, to be directed squarely at those who support the teaching of 'critical literacy' in high schools across the nation.

Yes, I was aware of this happening before I read Turner's essay, and indeed this is not the first time I have had something to say on the subject.[1] But Turner's intervention makes everything new again, given that it comes from the Director of the Centre for Critical and Cultural Studies at Queensland University and someone who is also a Federation Fellow of the Australian Research Council. Unlike many other critics of English teachers and subject English, Turner is both institutionally powerful and credible. Given his commitment to cultural studies and his standing in the field, moreover, he might reasonably have been expected to be on side with so-called critical literacy, if not also an ally of those who support and teach it. Indeed, in the *IJCS* piece, Turner justifiably claims credit himself for helping to re-make secondary-school English in the image of media and cultural studies, back in the early 1980s, in Western Australia. Why, then, is he turning on it now?

It seems the answer is that he feels his fifteen-year-old daughter's generation has been let down by his theoretical offspring, or by what teachers have allowed what he helped to create to become. The fiery blaze of the 'new' English that Turner helped to ignite in the 1980s has been hosed down by an educratic system that now offers students nothing more imaginative to write about than 'bloody Othering,' as he cites his daughter to bemoan (Turner 2007, 110)! Turner sees this as symptomatic of the 'mechanical and formulaically pre-emptive nature' of critical literacy approaches, which he maintains are focused on considerations of 'discourse,' 'politics' and 'ideology' at 'the exclusion of pleasure' (109–10).

But surely Turner is playing the role of the concerned parent disingenuously here, since he is not just any parent of a high school aged child. He is in fact (to use another of his impressive institutional titles) the immediate past president of the Australian Academy of the Humanities, who is also the author of many influential books in cultural studies that have helped to train a generation of university graduates (including many present-day English teachers) in critical approaches to discursive, political and ideological aspects of textuality. It is precisely in *this* role — as a leading figure in Australian and international cultural studies — that Turner's condemnation of subject English is remarkable and momentous. Why is it that Turner wants the critical literacy approaches taught in Australian high schools today to be seen as a *failed* project of university cultural studies? That, more or less, is a position one might attribute to callers on talk-back radio or bloggers on the Net. Why is an eminent cultural studies scholar expressing it — and in the guise of a concerned parent? What (and I don't mean psychologically) is going on here?

II

As Turner sees it, students, when they are not being institutional subjects (when they're not being 'students'), seek and derive pleasure from the consumption of cultural texts, and the English curriculum has forgotten to acknowledge this. With a view, then, to becoming more 'student-centred' (an aim Turner appears to regard as incontestable), the curriculum ought to develop a more 'responsive' approach to 'the students' own engagement with various media forms' (110). Out there in popular-culture land, away from the classroom, the kids just want to veg out in front of TV shows like *Everybody Loves Raymond.* It's only in the school environment that they're expected to pretend that everybody loves Raymond Williams.

On this view, what's wrong with critical literacy is that it fails to take account of people's real-life, organic forms of engagement with culture — as if subject English ought to be neither disciplinary nor institutional. The fantasy that, by contrast, somehow cultural studies is just unproblematically *of* what it studies, so that it doesn't so much 'study' culture as embody or describe it, seems to be the model that Turner wants subject English to aspire to. In this way, the problem with critical literacy, he argues, is not that it's a failed project of university cultural studies, but that it isn't really cultural studies at all. 'The "critical literacy" approach, as established in Australia, is a mode of discourse analysis,' Turner writes, 'developed by theorists from the discipline of Education and enthusiastically taken up by state education bureaucrats influenced by the branch of systemic linguistics identified with Sydney Professor M.A.K. Halliday' (106). Later he insists on the need to acknowledge 'significant distinctions between the approaches taken respectively by cultural studies, postmodernism and critical literacies' (106).[2] So while the air downunder may be thick with accusations levelled at subject English through the media and the parliaments, Turner wants it known that the sins of critical literacy are not the fault of cultural studies. The real offenders are the opportunistic 'educationists' who at some unspecified time in the recent past made over the 'new' English that Turner and others helped to devise in the 1980s into something based on 'a model of education that was more suited to the social sciences than the humanities' (111).

Such a distinction (between the prescriptive instrumentality of critical literacy and the organic vitality of cultural studies) recalls Lévi-Strauss's fanciful opposition in *The*

Savage Mind between so-called engineering discourse and bricolage. As Derrida (1978) has shown, that opposition doesn't hold.[3] Hence it is hardly surprising that the following passage from a classic cultural studies text, John Hartley's *Understanding News*, could easily be read as conforming to the terms which Turner uses to define critical literacy *against* cultural studies:

> Given that the capitalist mode of production continuously generates potential antagonism between classes, the acceptance of or submission to capitalist social relations is contingent upon the 'neutralization' of this antagonism. Capitalist societies are characterized by agencies such as the media, the family, education, the law and the State which, without removing the fundamental causes of potential class antagonism, translate it into other forms. None of these agencies could be effective on its own, but equally none of them can be understood adequately unless this aspect of their social function is analysed. (Hartley 1982, 56)

No doubt the (Marxist) allusion here to socially antagonistic forces risks derision as a crudely programmatic approach to an understanding of culture, but the book itself is scarcely 'formulaic' for making a thinly veiled reference to Marx. Marx's name, indeed, doesn't appear at all in *Understanding News*. Yet a quick check of the index shows as many entries listed for M.A.K. Halliday as for Stuart Hall (a leading figure in the development of 'British' cultural studies), Ferdinand de Saussure (founder of semiotics) and Russian linguist Vladimir Volosinov. By far the greatest number of entries, though, appears under 'discourse' (including the subset, 'news-discourse') and 'ideology,' and surely the only reason that 'politics' isn't listed is that to include it would have meant having to index every page. *Understanding News* is an undeniably political book, in other words, adopting an unashamedly oppositional stance towards conservative structures of power and sense in solidarity with the disenfranchised and the under-represented. But to see it therefore as instrumentally prescriptive would be to miss seeing that, because the book draws on such a discontinuous set of terms, ideas and arguments in response to various discursive, ideological and political problems associated with the interpretation of texts, it is also a work of bricolage.

Moreover, to see it as a work of cultural studies would be to miss seeing it as a work of critical literacy. What might be called the project of *Understanding News*, after all, is to get people to acknowledge the meaning-making effects and limitations of news production, or (as Hartley puts it) to see that 'news is a discourse generated by a general sign-system in relation to a social structure' (7). There can be no question that this is a critical project (which does not therefore preclude it from being a cultural studies project at the same time), the express aim of which is to help readers to become 'news-literate' (5). The point of the book, then, is not simply to interpret culture but to change it, an aim both critical and democratic. Democratic, in the sense Derrida means by democracy, as a *promise* we inherit from Marx and the Enlightenment and which we in turn are responsible for passing on to the future without seeking to pre-empt or predetermine what the future might bring (see Derrida 1994; and Lucy 2004, 14–25). No less than *Specters of Marx* or *The Communist Manifesto, Understanding News* is a book that is also an event, the event-ness of which is irreducible to a publication date or a particular act of reading.

In these terms, as a reaffirmation of the promise of democracy, who cares whether *Understanding News* is a work of 'cultural studies' or 'critical literacy'? What, indeed, is a humanities subject that doesn't always exceed the limits of a discipline if not also the very idea of disciplinarity as such, being always something other, more and larger than 'itself'?

For example: subject English.

III

English has always been, as I have said elsewhere, 'as a discipline, fairly undisciplined' (Lucy 1997, vii), so that while the turn to discourse, politics and ideology as key hermeneutic markers may be historically recent, it is not quite entirely new. Certainly it isn't new in the sense of a departure from 'core' pedagogy, since English has never really had one. It may indeed be, as Ian Hunter (1994) argues, that the ideal English graduate has always been imagined as a well-rounded, liberal-minded (or 'ethical') individual, but that is not to say there haven't been significant curricular changes over time in seeking to produce such an individual (see McIntyre 2001). Turner's complaint, then, that critical literacy is 'driven by a theoretical position where the end point is always already known in advance' (109) could in fact be levelled, on Hunter's argument, at any version of subject English from the past hundred years or so. For critical literacy to differ from those earlier versions, its 'theoretical position' would need to be of such an order that its projected 'end point' was other than the reproduction of ethical individuals.

So what is its theoretical position? Judging from the features ascribed to critical literacy at the website of the Tasmanian Department of Education, its position is broadly 'poststructuralist.' By this I mean that critical literacy is both explained and justified in terms of its relations to an 'outside' that cannot be separated from whatever might be argued to constitute its 'inside' in formal, technical or disciplinary terms. In a word, critical literacy is not really reducible to a 'discipline' at all:

> *What are the features of a critical literacy approach?*
> - We deconstruct the structures and features of texts. We ask questions of the text. We consider the structure and style of the text and ask: For what purpose has the text been constructed in this way?
> - We no longer consider texts to be timeless, universal or unbiased. Texts are social constructs that reflect some of the ideas and beliefs held by some groups of people at the time of their creation. As we examine the underlying values and consider the ways in which we, as readers and viewers, are positioned to view the world, we are able to develop opposing interpretations.
> - We explore alternative readings. We consider what has been included and what has been

left out. Which aspects of life does the author value? If we were to view the text from different perspectives, would we value those aspects, too? Does the text present unequal positions of power?

- We focus on the beliefs and values of the composer. We consider the time and culture in which the text was created. In what ways might the views represented in the text be similar to or different from the views that we hold today? Are there psychological, social, cultural and/or political reasons for the differences?

- We work for social equity and change. As we begin to analyse the powerful ways in which visual, spoken, written, multimedia and performance texts work and we discover the ways in which our feelings, attitudes and values are manipulated by language, we begin to operate powerfully within our world. We are able to become agents of social change working towards the removal of inequalities and injustices.

(Department of Education, Tasmania 2005)

Now of course the lofty aim of producing 'agents of social change' is open to ridicule for being impractical, in defence of which all that need be said is that every ideal risks this charge. The more damning accusation, though, would be that such an aim is not so much impractical as improper, which is why conservatives in the media, education and politics often characterise critical literacy as 'leftist': the more that critical literacy is made to seem like an ideological or a political program, the more it seems that subject English was once properly 'disinterested' and disinterestedly 'proper.'

This charge needs to be approached with caution, since it is not completely unfounded. While critical literacy is not 'Marxist' literacy, any more than *Understanding News* is *Understanding News According to Marx*, the aims both of critical literacy and Hartley's book cannot be dissociated from a certain idea of democracy as the always unfinished project of 'working towards the removal of inequalities and injustices' — an idea which could be said to encapsulate the spirit of Marx's work. In an era of bipartisan conservatism, however, Marx is a particular problem for what the right continues to refer to as 'the left,' given that conservatism has succeeded in making 'Marx' synonymous either with hard-line ideology or starry-eyed social theory (see Lucy and Mickler 2009). The problem for what the right still calls 'the left,' then, lies in knowing that what 'the left' means continues to be haunted by a relation to Marx which can never be exorcised. For this reason it is not the right, but only what the right today refers to as 'the left,' which is vulnerable to being called idealist when it comes to whatever now passes for what used to be known as its historical mission.

It is in this context that Turner's separation of cultural studies from critical literacy, it seems to me, makes sense. By siding with the condemnation of critical literacy in the media and the parliaments, cultural studies stands to win a certain respectability for itself by characterising critical literacy as its other. Hence it is entirely in the professional-institutional interests of university cultural studies to denounce secondary-school critical literacy, which it suits cultural studies to define as 'mechanical and formulaically pre-emptive' even at the cost of betraying its own history. Couched as an internecine squabble between not only supposedly different disciplines but also supposedly different levels of intellectual rigour, the bad copy that is critical literacy taught at high school cannot hope to match the authority of the good original in the form of cultural studies taught at university. Everything, then, depends on cultural studies coming before critical literacy, despite the fact that a seminal work of cultural studies like *Understanding News* draws on concepts, terms and arguments associated with what is now called critical literacy for much of its intellectual and political force. It is only by ignoring this fact (namely, that in fact critical literacy comes before cultural studies) that university cultural studies may presume to lecture secondary-school critical literacy on the latter's alleged lack of a sophisticated understanding of concepts, terms and arguments that university cultural studies does not own. 'The state school syllabus documents [concerning critical literacy] are full of embarrassingly garbled and just plain ham-fisted renditions of cultural, critical and media theory,' Turner writes, in seeming sympathy with the widely reported views of conservative commentators such as Luke Slattery and Kevin Donnelly, and so it is hardly surprising that 'such documents attract the attention of those who already regard the contemporary humanities as jargon-filled, "politically correct" posing' (108).[4] But what this objection obscures is the important question of why the authors of such documents might have chosen not to write them in so-called plain English (assuming the inference is not that they were incapable of doing so). Granted, some syllabus documents could no doubt be improved with retrospective editing, but surely this would be true of many papers in cultural studies as well. Surely cultural studies scholars, whose own writing has for many years been ridiculed as 'jargon-filled' by the likes of Slattery, Donnelly and others, are not now going to accuse advocates of critical literary of not being able to write well?

As for the claim that documents associated with critical literacy are not only badly written ('garbled') but also theoretically ill-informed ('just plain ham-fisted'), consider the features from the Tasmanian website listed above. Aside from a handful of terms ('deconstruct,' 'social constructs,' 'opposing interpretations,' 'alternative readings') which some might call jargon, the list is written in a way that is no more difficult to read than a newspaper article. With the possible exception of the reference to deconstruction, moreover, even the specialist or 'jargon' terms are scarcely intimidating. Yet while this may not be a difficult text to read in a straightforwardly functional sense, it doesn't follow that it must therefore be easy to understand. On the contrary, what might be called the ideas it espouses — especially the idea that all meaning is contextual and therefore irreducible to the intentions of an individual, thus putting even the very idea of the individual into context — are by no means uncontroversial, and indeed such ideas often meet with sometimes violent resistance and condemnation. The idea that, in a nutshell, 'there is nothing outside of the text' (Derrida 1976, 158) continues both to befuddle and to be laughed at more or less in equal measure, so seemingly counter-intuitive is it to entertain the possibility that things like truth, meaning and reality may not exist independently of the ways in which they are thought or represented to exist 'in themselves,' prior to (as it were) thinking or representation.

It can't be easy to try to teach this idea to high-school English students if the difficulty of trying to teach it to university undergraduates is anything to go by. But that is no reason not to try to teach it, and the Tasmanian Education Department website gives a perfectly good example (one that would not be out of place in *Understanding News*) of an in-class practical exercise that could be used for such a purpose. The exercise involves (in part) getting students to watch TV footage of a netball match and a game of Australian Rules football, paying attention to the textual feature of 'the camera techniques.' They would then be asked to consider the following questions:

> What kind of game do the camera shots suggest
> that it is?
> Which aspects of each game are ignored or
> focused on?
> Which telecast is more exciting to watch?
> Why?

Notice that the question of pleasure or excitement, far from being overlooked or excluded, is itself turned into a problem here. Rather than thinking of pleasure as innate or natural, students are asked to think about it as an effect of particular textual devices that need not be confined to camera angles in the present instance, but may include other production features such as lighting treatments and the use of audio. Nor does the exercise prescribe that pleasure must be understood in terms only of a response to forms of cultural entertainment, since surely it has to be allowed that a student could find it pleasurable simply to engage with (new) ideas. Some students, at least, may get pleasure just from doing the exercise itself.

Many others won't, of course. Yet the issue is not whether the exercise provides students with an opportunity to *experience* pleasure, but that it provides an opportunity for them to think about what pleasure 'is.' In this way, too, they are asked to think about how the different meanings associated with different sports might not be separable from, but rather utterly embedded in, particular televisual (and other) textual strategies and techniques. This would not be to suggest, however, that meanings are *determined* by contexts or by textual devices, since a particular camera shot might be interpreted quite differently by students in outback Kalbarri than by students in inner-city Kirribilli.[5] (Contextual 'limits' are always fluid and never fixed.) Moreover, since there is no outside the text, the exercise could lead to a discussion of gender issues (say) or to the representation or textualisation of 'others.' Students could be asked to consider, for example, whether differences between the textual treatments of women's netball and men's football are simply professional, or complexly (albeit not necessarily conspiratorially) discriminatory. Or they could be asked to look for textual evidence to support or contest the claim that Indigenous footballers and (I have no doubt) Indigenous netballers are treated in textually different ways from non-Indigenous players. This could lead in turn to a broader discussion not of racism understood in self-consciously 'moral' terms, but of what might be called popular race-based stereotyping.

Bloody othering? Bloody oath.

IV

So what could be wrong with this? Adopting a patrician tone from a disciplinary point of view (though 'disciplinary' is not at all the right word), one could complain that, on the evidence of the Tasmanian website, critical literacy uses 'deconstruction' in a fairly reductive sense to mean something like a method or an analytical approach. It would be all too easy to accuse this of being 'wrong' by citing Derrida's many objections to thinking of deconstruction as a method, a discipline, a mode of critique or a form of critical practice (see Lucy 2004, 11–14). But so what? If the official educational objective of subject English were that students should develop an understanding of what might be meant by 'deconstruction' which would meet with university-level approval, then there may well be grounds for advising that syllabus documents and teaching resources could do with a bit of a re-write. Ironically, though, any attempt to reproduce someone's idea of the 'purity' of deconstruction would always already be open to many possible deconstructive rejoinders, so that in a sense the claim that subject English 'misunderstands' deconstruction could never be made in the name of deconstruction. Attempts to partition deconstruction from its 'outsides' would always risk taking the form of a kind of intellectual apartheid, as Derrida (1985) argued a long time ago (see also Lucy 1995, 1–21), a risk that any appeal to the 'purity' or 'essence' of a thing entails. If, in other words, cultural studies did not set itself up in professional-institutional *opposition* to critical literacy, it might not be trying to teach critical literacy to suck eggs.

Instead of seeing critical literacy as a 'discipline' with the allegedly narrow aim of promoting the interests of Hallidayan linguistics, it ought to be possible to respond to it as a broadly conceived project or quasi-enterprise belonging (without belonging) to what Derrida (1994) calls 'the new international.' Like the essence of a poem, the essence of the new international is that it doesn't have one. Its limits, then, are indeterminate, approximating something like a positive form only in the conservative denunciation of whatever questions the authority of 'proper' ways of thinking and the 'proper' order of things (Lucy 2004, 80–5). It's for this reason that conservatives are opposed, more or less interchangeably and with equal force, to critical literacy, cultural studies, postmodernism, deconstruction, feminism, multiculturalism, Marxism, 'black armband' history and ... whatever else they see as an affront to nature and tradition 'imagined,' in the words of a John Kinsella (2008) poem, 'as consistency/and moral equilibrium.'

V

None of this should be taken to mean, it ought to go without saying, that critical literacy can't be improved upon or that it should be immune to criticism for being a 'project' rather than a discipline. But it has to be acknowledged that those who teach critical literacy at high school, as distinct from those who teach cultural studies or deconstruction (or postmodernism, or whatever) at university, teach it to a cohort which is neither self-selecting nor voluntary. Universities enjoy the privilege of pretending that their intakes are 'classless,' because students who enrol at university do so by choice and on the basis of having achieved a fancifully 'standard' entrance requirement. While academics know that in fact there are many differences among students in the courses they teach, they can justify overlooking those differences on the presumption that all students enrolled in a university course have proven themselves to be more or less equally capable of passing it. Besides, differences among university undergraduates rarely take the form of students telling the lecturer to 'go fuck yourself!' They rarely result in students, individually or in large numbers, threatening the lecturer with dangerous implements, throwing rocks at the lecturer, wilfully damaging the lecturer's car, punching the lecturer in the face or getting their parents to issue the lecturer with a death threat. These and other incidents (the non-ironic forms of which have all been recounted to me by high-school English teachers) do occur in the secondary sector, however, and in some cases (depending on socio-economic and other factors) they happen in some schools routinely. This is not to say, of course, that such incidents typify the sector, as though all secondary-school English teaching were combative. Certainly they are not typical of teaching environments in private schools, which have greater freedom than public schools to expel unwanted students and generally to monitor and modify the selection of their intakes. But any debate about secondary education that fails or refuses to acknowledge the many social, economic, behavioural, cultural and other differences within the sector, cannot be a debate about education. It may be a political or an ideological debate, but it cannot be an education debate *unless* it is willing to go beyond the text. Education, in a word, is never simply a 'theory.'

I've taught literature courses at many Australian universities and I'm on record as saying that my one (representative) wish is that students might learn to appreciate that the governess in Henry James's *The Turn of the Screw* is undecidably mad *and* that she see ghosts, and that there is no a priori, transcendental reason for having to choose between these supposedly different readings (see Lucy 2001, 77–96 'Catholic English'). But this is a kind of classless, 'Kirribilli' wish that perhaps only the coordinator of a university literature unit could afford to indulge. In a group of some twenty to thirty students, moreover, the wish may even stand a realistic chance of coming true. But the state secondary-school English programs are taught to thousands of students at a time, soon to become tens of thousands as the recently elected Labor Government rolls out its national curriculum. Before university lecturers start telling high-school teachers what to teach, then, they should probably consider that what 'teaching' means in a university environment may not be equivalent to its meaning in a high-school classroom, especially not one in which students seem to think that chairs were made for throwing rather than for sitting on. In a university seminar, the teaching experience is always likely to be a lot more 'Kirribilli' than 'Kalbarri'; and although some universities enjoy better resources, and better funding, than others, infrastructural differences within the sector are less undemocratic than in the school system. Before there are thought to be significant 'disciplinary' differences between critical literacy and cultural studies, in other words, it must be accepted that these subjects are taught at present under very different conditions.

The uneven, undemocratic distribution of resources and opportunities in the secondary sector can never hope to be redressed by attempts to refine or perfect subject English as a 'discipline,' though of course it suits conservatives in government and the media to scandalise that subject's disciplinarity as a way of distracting attention from the manifest inequalities and injustices in the sector caused by, among other explanations, inadequate funding. How, in short, does equity stand to be improved by condemning critical literacy (as many of its detractors seemingly delight in doing) for not endorsing 'the notion that "qualities of literature" can be equated with "life" values' (Lucy and Coroneos 1990, 53)? The authority of such an equation (between forms of representation generally and a thing called 'life') has pretty much been under constant questioning since at least the infamous emergence of structuralism in the 1960s and '70s in the English-speaking West (see Lucy 2002). The resistance to it in Australia today is therefore nothing new. As with the earlier attacks on structuralism, today's tabloid-style campaign against poststructuralism is conducted by critics whose every word reveals what they are only too quick to presume to discredit in advance. When it comes to 'garbled' and 'ham-fisted,' how could you go past the postings of Kevin Donnelly's cheer squad at the Western Australian blogsite PLATO ('People Lobbying Against Teaching Outcomes') or Donnelly's own grammatically chaotic, not to mention conceptually problematic, *Dumbing Down* (2007)?[6] Feigning an air of superiority again, one might accuse both the advocates and the opponents of critical literacy of lacking a sophisticated understanding of the subject. But this would itself fail to understand that the interests of both sides are not the same. If a high-school English teacher were said to misunderstand 'the' meaning of deconstruction, for example, it would still need to be acknowledged that he or she was using it, albeit not necessarily self-consciously, in the context of 'working towards the removal of inequalities and injustices.' He or she would be using (or allegedly misusing) 'deconstruction' as a critical tool of the new international, organised (without being organised) around 'a link of affinity, suffering and hope' (Derrida 1994, 85). In its (non-institutional, non-prescriptive) affiliation with an idea of democracy, in other words, critical literacy understands the purpose of a humanities education to have something to do with the production or inspiration of 'agents of social change.' Such a purpose exceeds but may not preclude the need for subject English to meet with the approval of university cultural studies, or Derrida scholars.

But when someone like Slattery or Donnelly uses 'deconstruction' in a way that clearly indicates they have no idea what they are talking about, the interests served by their refusal to engage with deconstruction before condemning it are entirely consistent with those of conservatism's historical antagonism to critical thought. What conservatism can tolerate least of all in regards to critical literacy is not the latter's unwillingness to affirm the piety of Shakespeare, but its refusal to reproduce the kind of subject for whom the piety of Shakespeare is a guarantee of universal moral equilibrium. The ideal conservative subject of subject English, then, is not simply the liberal individual, but rather the liberal neo-evangelist for whom the collapse of the Soviet Union marks the end of ideology and the historical triumph of the liberal self. In the aftermath of that event, the problem for conservatives is that 'the left' continues to linger but not in official, parliamentary forms. It lingers — no longer even in the name of 'the left,' but in the formless form of the new international — through such affirmations as the Tasmanian Education Department's declaration that critical literacy is 'working towards the removal of inequalities and injustices.' It lingers in the form of critical literacy's reaffirmation of the promise of democracy, which cannot be thought to have been realised when the Soviet politburo became the Russian parliament. It lingers, and because of this it cannot be thought that 'the left' and 'ideology' are defined by meanings associated with the Soviet Union and especially not by the USSR's association with 'Stalinism.' It lingers, because inequalities and injustices remain to be redressed.

It is only against this background that the vehemence of the conservative hostility towards critical literacy makes sense. And it is precisely against this background that the 'disciplinarity' of critical literacy matters not a shred, at least not in advance of the question of which side critical literacy is on in the conflict between (as *Understanding News* reminds us to call them) socially antagonistic forces.

But since there can be no question that critical literacy is on the side of democracy against conservatism, then perhaps the question that remains is this: which side is Graeme Turner's cultural studies on?

3. THE WAR ON ENGLISH: AN ANSWER TO THE QUESTION, WHAT IS POSTMODERNISM? *(WITH STEVE MICKLER)*

This essay derives from our keynote address to the NSW English Teachers' Association Conference ('Licence to Thrill') in Sydney, December 2007. It is intended as an evidence-based rejoinder to widespread attacks on the alleged parlous state of secondary-school English in Australia today, where the problem seems to be that English has been taken over by 'postmodernism.' In this way postmodernism is seen as the general or foundational problem, and so it follows that 'postmodern' English must be a problem too.

Our first task, then, is to decide what 'postmodernism' means, according to its detractors. What are its alleged key features? This question occupies the initial section of the essay, which includes a series of counter arguments in response to what postmodernism is supposed to be guilty of 'undermining' or 'destroying.' In section two we move to a discussion of particular problems associated with so-called 'postmodern' English, before focusing (in section three) on the widely reported views of a strident adversary of contemporary English studies: Kevin Donnelly. Our comments here are confined to a discussion of Donnelly's most recent book, *Dumbing Down* (2007), which we take for a mature and considered expression of his approach to education. We conclude by way of pondering the question, whose interests are served by attacking postmodernism?

1. Postmodernism

Postmodernism is denounced for consisting (allegedly) of five broad features, all of which are meant to be equally damning:

- postmodernism holds there to be *no such thing as truth*
- postmodernism equals *moral relativism*
- postmodernism is *leftist*
- postmodernism is *anti-liberal*
- postmodernism holds there to be *no such thing as history.*

Under postmodernism, as historian Keith Windschuttle puts it, 'the pursuit of something as objective as the truth becomes a mere pipe dream' (Windschuttle 2007). So ingrained is this assumption — that for postmodernism there is *no such thing as truth* — that *Sydney Morning Herald* journalist Miranda Devine refers to 'a destructive era of postmodern truth-twisting' in one of her columns (Devine 2004), without feeling obliged to explain what she means by that expression. It comes as no surprise therefore that another newspaper columnist, Giles Auty, should accuse postmodernism of disillusioning the nation's youth by teaching them to disrespect the truth:

> Since the advent of postmodernism almost every worthwhile certainty and traditional virtue has not just been called into question but has come under increasing assault — usually in our centres of further education and supposed enlightenment. When the concepts of truth, honour, objectivity, altruism, justice and religious faith are treated with contempt or scepticism by those who instruct our young, is it any great wonder that some of the young should seek refuge in oblivion or narcolepsy? (Auty 2000)

On the subject of postmodernism's alleged equation with moral relativism, Clive Hamilton, former director of the self-styled 'progressive' Australia Institute in Canberra, writes:

> The error of post-modernism, which grew out of the broad academic Left and now dominates Western society, is that it has no metaphysical foundation for a moral critique. Without a metaphysics that is common to humanity, any moral stance must be relative and therefore be contestable and lacking in conviction. (Hamilton 2006)

Or as current Prime Minister Kevin Rudd, writing in the *Monthly* for October 2006, sees it, postmodernism has joined with secular humanism to supplant orthodox religious faith:

The impact of independent scientific enquiry, the increasing impact of secular humanism itself, combined with the pervasive influence of modernism and postmodernism, have had the cumulative effect of undermining the influence of the mainstream Catholic and Protestant churches across the West.

Where this will lead as Christianity enters its third millennium, remains to be seen. But there are signs of Christianity seeing itself, and being seen by others, as a counterculture operating within what some have called a post-Christian world. (Rudd 2006)

As for the claim that postmodernism is 'leftist,' Hamilton says as much above. But perhaps no one has put it so raucously as Auty, for whom postmodernism 'represents an attempt to usher in a new kind of left-wing totalitarianism via the unlocked back doors of democracies. Postmodernism represents the neo-Marxist conquest of Western cultures by stealth' (Auty 2000). Given the sometime hysterical tenor of these charges it is clear that whatever postmodernism is said to be, it is taken for a force (albeit one as insubstantial as a cloud, but which none the less 'dominates' the West) whose nature is excessive ('monstrous,' 'unnatural') and violent. Hence it goes without saying that postmodernism is *anti-liberal*, given its unbalanced views on truth and its 'dominating,' 'totalitarian' tendencies. Small wonder that it should also stand accused of adopting an extreme position in regards to history, the substance of which — according to

Windschuttle — it turns into a contest of 'political' stances and 'subjective' opinions:

> Academic historians have argued that the attempt to distance themselves from their own political system cannot be done. According to many, history is 'inescapably political.' In tandem with this has come the notion that history cannot be objective because there are no independent vantage points from which one can look down on the past. We can only see the world through the lenses of our own culture, so what we see is inherently subjective. And if that is so, then the pursuit of something as objective as the truth becomes a mere pipe dream. And we have to give up the idea of truth as an absolute concept and substitute a relative idea of truth. Under this notion, different cultures and even different political positions each have their own truths, even if they are incompatible with the truths of other cultures. This stance generally goes under the name of postmodernism. (Windschuttle 2007)

In order to attack postmodernism, from the left or the right, some version of the features we've identified has to be believed. The case against it rests, in other words, on an uncritical acceptance of the charges, based on the assumption that postmodernism inaugurates a radical break with so-called 'traditional' values and reason. These, however, are not traditional in a *timeless* sense, having their origins in the

European Enlightenment of the eighteenth century to which we owe the possibility of critiquing the very idea of tradition itself, along with notions of 'received wisdom,' 'absolute truth,' 'traditional values,' 'universal morality' and all forms of authority in general. In this light, 'postmodernism' marks simply the ongoing project (by other means, as it were) of such critique — or of that tradition.

Seemingly, then, the issue is not so much what postmodernism 'is,' but what it is used to *represent*. So how might it be represented differently from the professed features outlined above?

Postmodernism holds there to be no such thing as truth

Postmodernism represents a continuation (by other means) of a critical project associated with the Enlightenment, a project encapsulated in Kant's motto: *'Sapere Aude!'* — *dare to know* (Kant 1970, 54). It is therefore not an attack on 'truth' as such, but rather on notions of *absolute* truth as determined by the church or other institutions. (Since we no longer take it to be true that a woman's place is in the home, that all swans are white or that the poor are morally inferior to the rich, why should we take it as true that all texts have 'natural' or 'essential' meanings?) Since the Enlightenment opens the possibility of a critical scepticism towards received, official, orthodox, traditional, absolute or objective forms of truth and authority, this alleged feature of postmodernism turns out to be nothing less than a central feature of the Enlightenment.

Postmodernism equals moral relativism

Morality is another form of absolute universal truth; therefore the Enlightenment gives us a responsibility to rethink or challenge it. This results in the substitution of secular for religious morality, but on the understanding that secular morality (or 'ethics') cannot be taken as *absolute*. It too remains open to critique. (If morality is a fixed set of answers, ethics is an open set of questions. The one demands obedience, the other responsibility.) We can say, then, that the Enlightenment is on the side of philosophy versus theology, which is not to say that such an opposition is not always at the same time political. (It would be a gross insult to modern educators to expect them to accept the proposition that if they're not religious, they must be 'amoral' or 'relativist.') Again, an alleged feature of postmodernism turns out to be another central feature of the Enlightenment.

Postmodernism is leftist

Postmodernism is not a leftist 'program,' but it is a 'critical' project. Since critical thought can lead to social reform, then historically conservatism has always been opposed to it. Conservatives denounce 'postmodernism' as 'leftist,' then, because they *cannot* denounce it as 'critical' (this would be unsayable). Hence the attack on postmodernism is ultimately anti-intellectual (consider the import of this for debates about education, for example) and at the same time undemocratic, insofar as democracy depends less on free trade than it does on free thought. If it is 'postmodern' to ask after the conditions under which the meaning of a text might be said to occur, it is therefore also *democratic* to do so. Yet again: to the extent that the Enlightenment is a critical-intellectual project, post-modernism shares an essential feature with it.

Postmodernism is anti-liberal

We owe the notion of liberalism to the Enlightenment, particularly in terms of a tolerance for difference and a healthy scepticism towards absolute truth and unquestionable authority. Challenging the so-called 'natural' order of things made it possible, for example, to recognise racist, sexist and homophobic attitudes as unjust and undemocratic, and therefore to oppose them. So if it is 'postmodern' to question the 'natural' or 'essential' meaning of a text, such an attitude must be seen as belonging also to a *liberal* tradition of critical inquiry. If this attitude belongs to postmodernism, too, then postmodernism cannot be separated from the Enlightenment.

Postmodernism holds there to be no such thing as history

Postmodernism questions the nature of history (which follows from questioning the nature of truth), by asking for example who has the authority to *write* history and to make it into *official* history? These are professionally appropriate questions for modern historians to ask. To see them as 'radical' would be to invoke a notion of *absolute* truth, which produces history as a single narrative independent of anyone's critical relations to it. The social and political systems for which history is understood as a *single, pre-given* narrative of the truth are either religious or totalitarian. Note that both of these are opposed to critical thought. Once again, finally, in its questioning of history, postmodernism can be seen as continuing the critical project — or the tradition — of the Enlightenment.

2. Postmodern English

It follows from this that so-called 'postmodern' English is an outcome of secular, enlightened, modern critical thought. 'Postmodern' English dares to know.

But this is not how its detractors represent it. Those who oppose it associate postmodern English (often in the guise of 'critical literacy') with the following pejorative features:

- postmodern English is *anti-realist*
- postmodern English equals *moral relativism*
- postmodern English says there is *no such thing as truth*
- postmodern English uses *impenetrable jargon*
- postmodern English is *ideological*
- postmodern English is *anti-canonical.*

As education journalist Luke Slattery puts it, contemporary English studies is underpinned by 'an anti-realist theory of knowledge at odds with commonsense, as well as scientific and philosophical notions of truth: parents should be made aware of this, as should teachers who are not already' (Slattery 2005a). The mere assertion of the charge that postmodern English is 'anti-realist,' then, is enough to make this seem self-evidently alarming. Likewise it is enough just to *say* that postmodern English promotes 'moral relativism,' together with the idea that there is *no such thing as truth*, for such claims to arouse immediate concern. How else to respond to Donnelly's thesis in *Dumbing Down*, for example, that school leavers are 'ethically challenged as a result of a post-modern curriculum that teaches that values are subjective and that there is no such thing as truth as learning is a "socio/cultural construct"' (Donnelly 2007, 8)?

The claim that postmodern English is anti-realist or anti-commonsensical goes hand in glove with the accusation that its reliance on 'impenetrable jargon' is an abuse of plain language. That's why Queensland Labor Education Minister Rod Welford vowed to purge postmodernism from the English curriculum in his State — because of its 'mumbo jumbo.' 'It's really not a very constructive pathway for English learning at school,' he is reported to have said. 'Nothing will leave this department that I don't understand' (cited in Slattery 2005b)! Former Federal Education Minister Brendan Nelson took a similar view, accusing postmodernism of 'spreading cryptic jargon' throughout the secondary-school sector by way of university education departments — on which postmodernism has acted like a 'virus' (cited in Norrie 2005).

Just as its critical vocabulary is dismissed as 'mumbo jumbo,' so too are the critical aims of contemporary English studies ridiculed as grossly 'ideological' or 'politically correct.' This is a common charge, often coupled with postmodern English's alleged disrespect for the canon. 'I share the views of many people about the so-called postmodernism,' John Howard is reported to have said in 2006. 'I just wish that independent education authority didn't succumb on occasions to the political correctness that it appears to succumb to' (cited in Welch, 2006). Or as Brendan Nelson is quoted as putting it a year earlier: university education faculties have become 'in essence quasi-sociology departments' in which undergraduates study '*Buffy the Vampire Slayer* and those sort of things,' but not Milton 'and stuff like that' (cited in Norrie 2005). Summing up the case against postmodern English, former prime minister Howard was in no doubt that there are only two kinds of books in the world — 'high-quality literature' and 'rubbish.' 'We need a curriculum,' he said, 'that encourages an understanding of the high-quality literature and not the rubbish' (cited in Welch 2006).

Such are the charges against English studies in Australia today, which Donnelly develops at length in *Dumbing Down*. We now turn to a discussion of that book in response to accusations above.

3. *Dumbing Down*

Donnelly's book was officially launched by then prime minister John Howard at Parliament House, Canberra, in February 2007. The occasion, perhaps, recalls a form of patronage that was common in pre-Enlightenment times, given that the book in question was neither written by a celebrated author nor published by a distinguished press. So why did Howard choose to launch it — and at Parliament House? Certainly Donnelly (an executive director of a private education consultancy based in Melbourne) is well known as a media commentator on education, but that hardly accounts for the prime ministerial fanfare accompanying the book's release. Nor could Howard be thought to have regarded the book as a model of good communication in an increasingly 'illiterate' age of 'facile' email and mobile phone correspondence, given — as historian Stuart Macintyre points out — that *Dumbing Down* 'reveals an inability to construct a sentence' (Macintyre 2007). On the plentiful evidence presented by Macintyre of Donnelly's many grammatical and other errors, indeed, *Dumbing Down* would appear to meet all the criteria of what Howard calls 'rubbish' books.

But Howard was adamant that *Dumbing Down* is on the side of 'high-quality literature,' even if he stopped short of calling the book an example of it:

> I would commend to all of you Kevin's work on the way in which the teaching of English has been allowed in some cases to drift into a relativist wasteland, where students are asked to deconstruct texts using politically-correct theories in contrast with the traditional view that great literature has something profound to say about the human condition.
>
> In tackling these issues, often against the grain of self-proclaimed education 'experts,' Kevin Donnelly displays both great courage and a tough-minded determination to defend the higher purposes of education, especially in carrying forward the best of the Western cultural tradition. (Howard 2007)

Never mind, then, that Donnelly's sentences may be in want of some attention, what matters is that *Dumbing Down* champions the values and standards of 'the Western cultural tradition.' The conceit could scarcely be more unambiguous or startling: if we do not tend to that tradition, the future will turn into a 'wasteland.'

This, too, is Donnelly's argument in *Dumbing Down*. It is also a popular argument, of course, widely disseminated throughout the media, in parliament and across the public sphere. It appears frequently (for example) on the PLATO blogsite, the online forum of the group in Western Australia that calls itself 'People Lobbying Against Teaching Outcomes' (where 'outcomes' stands for 'outcomes-based education' and where many of the 'people' are English teachers), to which Donnelly often contributes and where he figures predominantly as the brave defender of 'standards' that Howard makes him out to be. It would be a mistake to dismiss Donnelly's views as ineffectual, then, simply because his prose falls short of being 'high-quality literature.' Donnelly's lack of distinction as a writer is not the issue. What matters (and here we agree with Howard) is precisely that Donnelly is represented, and frequently represents himself, as a champion of the values and standards of 'the Western cultural tradition' in defiance of the destructive force of 'postmodernism,' whose 'mantra,' Donnelly contends, is 'that knowledge is "socially and historically constructed"'(77). (The obvious inference here is that postmodernism should be scorned for not thinking that all knowledge is 'absolute' and 'transcendental.') For this reason *Dumbing Down* is an important text, we think, because the case it puts on behalf of those values and standards is a pastiche of popular arguments in favour of 'tradition' and popular anxieties surrounding 'postmodernism.' While Donnelly's take on these is undeniably idiosyncratic at times, all the same his book is a remarkable assemblage of otherwise unremarkable prejudices, moral panics and ill-founded assumptions in the service of what are ultimately undemocratic interests.

Donnelly uses 'postmodernism' as a collective term for whatever he sees — 'feminism,' 'deconstruction,' 'multiculturalism,' 'critical literacy,' 'the cultural left,' 'the New Age,' 'Marxism' and so on — as a threat to what he calls the 'liberal-humanist' or (as he puts it, wrongly) 'liberal/humanist' worldview belonging to the West, based on absolute values and knowledge. Those opposing this worldview, on Donnelly's reckoning, 'claim it is mono-cultural and that it reinforces a narrow, doctrinaire view of the world associated with Australia's Anglo/Celtic past' (184). But Donnelly thinks to have the perfect riposte:

> anyone familiar with the development of Western civilisation will know that it has drawn on a host of wider cultural influences. One only needs to look at the English language to note the impact of ancient Greek and Latin as well as remnants of the languages of the Vikings and the Normans. Many classical English myths and fables are derived from Europe, Arabia and India, and literature has long since stopped being the preserve of white, middle-class elites committed to King and country. Anyone who has walked through the British Museum will also know, that while England is unique as a country and it has evolved in a distinctive way, that it has drawn upon and absorbed a host of wider cultural influences. (184)

The problem with this retort, however, is that it defines, in ways both ridiculous and revealing, 'Western civilisation' as 'Anglo/Celtic.' Greeks, Latins, Vikings and Normans, it seems, are somehow *outside* influences on 'Western' civilisation. What manner of Anglo-centrism is barely disguised here? Against its own intentions, then, the passage is an object lesson in the consequences of a 'narrow, doctrinaire view' of the world — a case study of the very 'mono-culturalism' its author claims his position does *not* represent.

A further problem for Donnelly's argument is that the tradition of 'liberal-humanist' education he valorises appears to have two origins. It goes back a few hundred years (to a time he nominates as 'the rise of Western civilisation') *and* it goes back several thousand years, all the way to Ancient Greece. So the modern curriculum 'centred on particular subjects like mathematics, history and English,' he maintains, is owed to 'a view of education closely associated with the rise of Western civilisation that can be traced back over some hundreds of years' (177). Presumably he's referring to the European Enlightenment here, which would make his general point uncontentious. But Donnelly wants to draw a far longer bow:

> Since the time of the early Greek philosophers and sophists, evolving over the centuries and incorporating aspects of the Judeo/Christian tradition and historical movements such as the Renaissance, the Reformation and the Enlightenment, a liberal/humanist view of education is concerned — to use Matthew Arnold's expression — with 'getting to know, on all matters which most concern us, the best which has been thought and said' (Arnold 1969, p. 6). (Donnelly 2007, 177)

There is only one word — *revisionist* — to describe this approach to cultural history. The idea that the Ancient Greeks were liberal humanists simply is preposterous, serving to show that by 'liberal humanism' Donnelly means to invoke a notion of *timeless* values and standards that are absolute and foundational.[1] This allows him to think of history — to construct it — as a *single* narrative, a perfect continuum (albeit while conceding some vague 'evolutions') from the Greeks through to Renaissance England and on to twenty-first century Australia! On such a view, the entire cultural history of the West is but a serial repetition of its origin (its 'first' origin, as it were) in Ancient Greece, making it inconceivable that Australia, say, or for that matter England, could develop a cultural identity of its own. The irony of the 'history is continuous' thesis is that all historical differences have to be overlooked in order to believe that 'civilisation' was born in Ancient Greece, and that it has remained unchanged ever since. If this were so then the Enlightenment, far from having a distinctive identity, would be nothing more than another repetition of history's (original) 'origin.' Instead of being understood as a reaction to pre-modern, feudal authority vested in the church, the monarchy and the aristocracy, the Enlightenment could be seen only as a revisionist reaffirmation of values and standards deriving from Ancient 'liberal-humanist' Greece.

Hence, we surmise: Donnelly opposes 'postmodern' English because it disallows the 'history is continuous' thesis, which assumes an uninterrupted lineage from Shakespeare, for instance, to us. But to argue against that line, to argue that 'Shakespeare' is a text remaining open to occasional and periodic re-evaluations, is not to be committed to insisting that *Hamlet* is equivalent to a comic strip, a piece of graffito or (to use one of Donnelly's examples) 'a reality TV show' (Donnelly 2007, 158). The kinds of ludicrous interpretations misattributed to 'postmodernism' exist, that is to say, *only* in their misattributions.

More problematic still for Donnelly is that history's real (or truly original) origin turns out not to be Ancient Greece after all, but the Garden of Eden. We gave up trying to count how many times the neologism 'Judeo/Christian' appears in *Dumbing Down*; suffice to say, though, that it appears often enough to be conspicuous. The irony here is that it's precisely in reaction to Judeo-Christian teachings, according to which human history begins (and we become historical or 'fallen' beings) when Adam and Eve are flung from the Garden of Eden because Eve ate from the Tree of Knowledge, that Kant implores us to see that our historical future, as opposed to a mythological one, is tied to our capacity and willingness to *dare to know*. This turns history over to men and women to make of it what they decide, instead of condemning it to be endured as a punishment on the way to a 'better' world. The Enlightenment *breaks* with Judeo-Christian tradition, in short, and cannot be conflated with it. So much so that to the extent in which Judeo-Christian authority continues to exert a force today, we can say that we are still waiting for the Enlightenment to happen.

Against this, Donnelly conceives of history as a never-ending story — all the better to separate 'postmodernism' as perversely counter-historical. But for the postmodern 'wrong' turn, the history of the West would be just one long, unbroken line of near-perfect harmony:

> The reason for studying history is not simply so we are saved from repeating the same mistakes, equally as important is the recognition that, as individuals and as a society, we are involved in an unfolding narrative that began thousands of years ago and which continues to unfold into the future. Being part of that narrative promotes a

sense of belonging to something more lasting and significant than the often mundane routine of one's day-to-day existence. One of the strengths of a liberal/humanist view of education, in an era of social dysfunction, alienation and loss of meaning, is that there is a strong and life-affirming story about how Western civilisation has evolved and how, while being far from perfect, we are no longer ruled by superstition, bigotry and ignorance. (178)

Western civilisation isn't simply *different* from other cultures and civilisations, then; it is 'better' than them. But the idea that 'we' are better than 'them' can't hold together even in a single paragraph for Donnelly. On the one hand we (and the pronoun here is clearly not inclusive, say, of Indigenous Australians, though let's put this aside for now) are 'involved in an unfolding narrative' extending from thousands of years ago to today, when 'we are no longer ruled by superstition, bigotry and ignorance,' while on the other and at the same time we live in 'an era of social dysfunction, alienation and loss of meaning'! Hence we wonder whether what Donnelly really meant to say is that we live in 'an era of social dysfunction, alienation and loss of meaning' *because* 'we are no longer ruled by' religion, a belief in the cultural supremacy of the West and obedient acceptance of 'the' truth?

Donnelly's benighted advocacy of an anti-intellectual and pro-authoritarian position leaves us to surmise also that his objection to 'postmodern' English has to do with its affirmation — textually, ethically, historically, politically and so forth — of difference, dating from but not determined by the Enlightenment turn towards 'progressive' critique. Such affirmation may be no better represented today — no better reaffirmed — than in the ideas and methods developed under the rubric of 'critical literacy,' among the general aims of which is the development of students' critical skills with a view to lessening the chances of them being 'ruled by superstition, bigotry and ignorance.' What might be called the project of overcoming such anti-democratic forces remains unfinished, of course, as well as being both historically modern and discontinuous. For how could we ever have *enough* democracy?[2] Hence the authority of superstition today — through the church and other institutions and beliefs — is threatened by what Donnelly and other conservatives (such as Howard, Slattery, Windschuttle and the like), along with many on the left, call 'postmodernism,' because they *cannot* say it is threatened by the Enlightenment, modernity or a 'tradition' of critical thought.[3]

In this context, Donnelly's affirmation not of difference, but of Anglo-Celtic/Judeo-Christian authority, commits his critique of 'postmodern' English to a form of *cultural studies* — the very thing he accuses postmodern English of being. And what makes the Anglo-Celtic/Judeo-Christian heritage so 'superior,' according to Donnelly, if not its allegiance to principles of fairness, tolerance and diversity — the very things, again, that he accuses 'postmodernism' of promoting in the form of multiculturalism, anti-racism, egalitarianism and a critique of power relations? What so offends Dr Donnelly, we continue to surmise, is that what he calls 'postmodernism' is an affirmation of difference that is also therefore on the side of democracy:

Within the culture wars, clear thinking is re-badged as critical literacy and given a left-wing slant. Students, no longer taught how to identify and deal with different persuasive devices, such as generalisations and ad hominem arguments, are instead taught to analyse texts in terms of power relationships and what is considered politically correct, especially in areas such as gender, ethnicity and class. The Tasmanian website [of that State's education department], when outlining the benefits of critical literacy, suggests:

> *Critical literacy provides us with ways of thinking that uncover social inequalities and injustices. It enables us to address disadvantage and to become agents of social change.*
> Tasmanian Department of Education, 2005.

(Donnelly 2007, 147)

What exactly is supposed to be the problem here? That 'postmodern' English invites students to think about literature in terms of 'gender, ethnicity and class'? That it asks them to engage with literary and other kinds of texts as a way of thinking about 'social inequalities and injustices'? But since when have such questions been *postmodern*, as if to ask them were to take literary studies away from 'itself'? Could it be possible to read *Pride and Prejudice*, for instance, today or in the past, without seeing that social and sexual power in the world of that novel is gendered? Would it be wrong for 'postmodern' students to consider ways in which gender relations today differ from the social referents of Austen's novel, set in eighteenth-century provincial England? Would it be wrong for them to understand the context in which those relations might be seen to differ, as no less than historical through and through?

Only a revisionist approach to literary history could construct these questions as proof of a 'wrong' turn associated with postmodernism. For since when has literature not dealt with issues of 'gender, ethnicity and class'? Take Jonathan Swift's *A Modest Proposal*, for example, a text that Donnelly himself commends. Published in 1729, this satirical political pamphlet pushes at the limits of utilitarian reason by putting a rational case for solving the problem of famine among the 'over'-populated Irish poor of the time by getting them to eat their surplus young.[4] To contest this argument would be to do so *ethically*, asserting on behalf of a certain idea of what 'society' means that reason alone won't do. To read against the text's affirmation of rationality, then, would be to see at the very least that the utilitarianism it advocates depends on accepting *unequal* relations of ethnicity and class as *natural*. If the superiority of English landowners to the indentured Irish poor is *not* natural, however, then it must be historical and therefore able to be changed. So any argument (no matter how seemingly reasoned) for maintaining the status quo has to be seen as serving the interests of those who have power already — the English landowners — against those who don't, the Irish poor.

But Donnelly might want to raise an objection here, claiming that this reading operates on the basis of an unacknowledged 'slippage' from textual to extra-textual concerns. He might want to say that we've forgotten to read *A Modest Proposal* as a work of *literature*; that we've forgotten to see it as a set of 'persuasive devices' belonging to a work of fiction on behalf of an idea of the 'purely' literary. In that case we might want to ask how we could have arrived at our reading, except by taking account of the 'persuasive devices' that the text uses to promote unequal social relations as natural? Since when did reading texts 'in terms of power relationships,' in other words, not mean reading them in recognition of 'different persuasive devices' that may be used in an attempt to naturalise power — or to naturalise 'social inequalities and injustices'? Note that Donnelly's rhetorical trick (his persuasive device) here is to denounce something he otherwise approves of, by giving it another name. He denounces the analysis of 'power relationships,' but approves the analysis of what he calls 'persuasive devices.' Note too that Donnelly cannot quite get *outside* of modernity in order to condemn contemporary English studies' focus on — precisely — 'different persuasive devices,' since to do so it would be necessary to deny that English *should* be concerned with understanding those devices and instead become a quasi-religious project requiring students to believe rather than to think. For us, then, it would be perfectly legitimate (though of course Donnelly would disagree) to ask students to consider ways in which some of the persuasive devices used in *A Modest Proposal* might also be found, albeit in different forms and to varying degrees, in policy documents and other texts relating to Aboriginal people as inalienably 'other.' For us it would be entirely within the scope of English studies to read *A Modest Proposal* as a text employing certain persuasive devices on behalf of a *discourse* on race and class, and it goes without saying that this would not be to preclude many other possible readings.

Hence the textual/extra-textual distinction is problematic,

if not altogether false. Could it be that this is what Derrida was getting at when he wrote that 'there is nothing outside of the text' (Derrida 1976, 158)? There is nothing — no meanings, no inferences — outside of a *context*, in other words, since there could be no possibility of a transcendental, context-free zone within which a meaning or an inference could be said to occur. (Note it does not follow that if meanings are never independent of contexts, then context must *determine* meaning. But that's not quite the point for now.) One consequence of this is that literature loses its stability or inviolability as a concept, which is not to be committed to saying that there is *no such thing* as literature. Literature's 'identity,' then, is put in question, in company with the larger question of textuality in general, but again this is not to say that therefore literature has *no* identity at all.[5] The question of textuality invites, in turn, a consideration of many different kinds of textual forms, not all of which are necessarily 'literary' or even necessarily linguistic or print-based. None of these forms, including literary texts, is transcendental, since textuality is inseparable from a network — a text — of historical, technological, political, cultural and other forces and contexts. This is not to argue — far from it — that all forms of textuality are equivalent in aesthetic, discursive, affective, institutional and other ways. It does not follow from the recognition that textual meanings and values are never transcendental that, as Donnelly wrongly asserts, postmodernism is committed to teaching 'that all texts are of equal value' (158). So, too, the often repeated charge that English teachers today see *no* difference between an SMS message, for example, and a Shakespeare play, is a furphy used to make it seem that English teachers do not have a professional responsibility to introduce students to an understanding of the different persuasive and other devices at work across a range of contemporary textual forms. Hence the furphy is that teachers are not being 'professional' when they refer to texts other than literature; they are being 'ideological.' Because Jane Austen did not have a mobile phone to use or a cinema to go to, so the argument seems to be, then Australian teens in the twenty-first century have no need or right to be exposed to the formal study of the kinds of textuality made possible by technologies of the phone and cinema, whose development Austen could not have dreamt of.

A further consequence of the problematic nature of the text/outside-text distinction is that a concept such as the literary canon cannot be understood as absolute, a-contextual or transcendental. (So much for Howard's assertively transcendental distinction between 'high-quality' and 'rubbish' literature, a fuzzy division if ever there were.) But without an incontestably fixed and stable canon, the core of Donnelly's argument is at risk of meltdown. He has no choice, then, but to defend it, even while conceding that 'the' canon is subject to historical and other forms of change. What he wants us to believe does *not* change, however, is the concept or idea of the canon as such, without which much of Donnelly's attack on 'postmodern' English would lose its force. Unsurprisingly, since the modern concept of a canonical set of literary masterworks is associated powerfully with British critic and academic F.R. Leavis, writing from the late 1920s through to the early 1970s, Donnelly turns to Leavis for support:

> One of the main advocates of the more conservative approach [to literary criticism], the English critic F. R. Leavis, admitted that

the literary canon evolved over time and that students, far from being passive, should respond to literary texts in an engaging and active way:

> *In my account of what a due performance of the function of criticism would have been like — for there you have my theme — the conception of criticism I invoked was the very reverse of a dogmatic one ... criticism, of its essential nature, is collaborative — collaborative and creative, and that a due performance of the function requires a plurality of centres.* Leavis, 1956, p. 56 [in fact this passage appears on pp. 56–7]

(Donnelly 2007, 73–4)[6]

The problem for Donnelly here is that, unlike the Ten Commandments, the canon is open to disagreement, intervention and change, forcing him to acknowledge that even Leavis 'admitted that the literary canon evolved over time.' How could it not? In a secular, critical society, as opposed to an orthodox religious one, how could a concept like the canon *not* be subject to historical, aesthetic, cultural, political and other transforming effects? As the bedrock of English studies, then, the canon turns out to be about as solid as the air, its only 'permanent' feature being that it is permanently subject to transformation. Some of the poets, for example, whom Leavis sought to induct into the canon through his first important book, *New Bearings in English Poetry*, first published in 1932, are seldom read at all today, posing the question of what a 'formerly' canonical work or writer might look like. How could a text or an author be a part of 'the' canon one day, and discarded the next?

So it would seem that the question of canonicity is a subject best left to cardinals and rabbis to decide, which secular literary critics would do well to leave alone. But if Donnelly's cooption of Leavis was never going to produce the desired effect of reinforcing an ideal of the canon as a *single, pre-given* set (a certain kind of narrative construction) of 'high-quality' literary works, a further problem for Donnelly is that the picture he paints of Leavis as a 'conservative' is not entirely straightforward either. Certainly Leavis took what would be called today a conservative view on art and literature, so that for him 'great' artistic and literary works do not simply represent the moral life of the times in which they were produced — they *embody* that life. Even so, if a conservative critic is someone who looks only to the past for moral and aesthetic reassurance, Leavis went far beyond type in maintaining an active interest in the new. He may not have been always enthusiastic about new writing, but he was at least always interested in what was being written; and this, the principle of curiosity as it might be called, is something he sought to inspire in his students. He encouraged them to read Joyce's *Ulysses*, for instance, although Leavis himself cantankerously disapproved of the book. Nor can it be overlooked that Leavis insisted (as indeed Donnelly quotes him to say) that criticism emanates from 'a *plurality* of centres.'

But while Donnelly is keen to enlist Leavis in support (as he must think) of his argument, he appears reluctant to emulate him. Unlike Leavis, Donnelly has no stomach for the new. Instead of being curious as to what might be going on in English studies today, instead of daring to know what it might have to offer, Donnelly dismisses it out of hand. Everything for him about the contemporary study of literature is 'extra'-literary and therefore improper according to an ideal of literary studies as he imagines it was taught in the past. Because English today is not supposedly what it used to be, therefore it must be condemned. Because there has been change, therefore it must be turned back. Because contemporary English studies sees the distinction between textual and 'extra'-textual fields as a problem, thus opening it to a consideration of many different kinds of literary and other texts, therefore it is not English studies. Therefore it must have turned into an ideological, anti-canonical, anti-realist, morally relativist, counter-historical program run by the left, with the aim of bringing civilisation as we know it — *Western* civilisation — to an end by using obtuse jargon to indoctrinate young people into thinking there is no such thing as truth! English, in a word, has been made over into *cultural studies*, and the calamitous effects attending this transformation are not confined to Australia:

> It is worth noting that Australia is not alone in the way literature has been transformed into cultural studies, where students are taught to analyse texts in terms of power relationships and as examples of how those more powerful in society are able to exert control. As noted by the US academics Patai and Corral, literature has been under attack throughout the English-speaking world:
>
> > *What theorists of all these persuasions* [known collectively as 'postmodernists'] *have in common, whatever their individual differences, is a decisive turning away from literature as literature and an eagerness to*

> *transmogrify it into a cultural artefact (or
> 'signifying practice') to be used in waging an
> always anti-establishment ideological political
> struggle.* Patai and Corral 2005, p. 8.
> (Donnelly 2007, 154)[7]

Again, Donnelly seems to have quoted others against the best interests of his argument. For what is the call that Donnelly makes throughout *Dumbing Down* — for affirmative action on behalf of the Anglo-Celtic/Judeo-Christian literary and cultural tradition — if not a plea for literature to be seen not 'as' literature, but as 'a cultural artefact'? Notice too (and not for the first time) the implicit denigration of an otherwise seemingly unextraordinary aim of English studies, in this case that of teaching literature as an example 'of how those more powerful in society are able to exert control.' What would be the problem with this? Think again, for example, of Swift's *A Modest Proposal*, which presents not merely a 'literary' critique of Anglo ruling-class abuses perpetrated on the Celtic peasant class, but also and unashamedly an ethical and a political critique. Why should students be prevented from engaging with this text today, engaging with its 'persuasive devices,' other than as an example of 'literature as literature'? *A Modest Proposal* was published originally, after all, as a *political* pamphlet. How come we should be constrained to think of it now *only* as a work of literature?

Once more, then, we surmise: Donnelly wants us to think of literature (and in this he is vastly at odds with Leavis's project) as a transcendental category, a-contextually free of history, gender, class, ethnicity, politics, sexuality, desire and other 'external' factors and forces. Against this, however, he tries to persuade us at the same time that (at the very least) history, culture and ethnicity are bound inextricably to a notion of *English* literature, such that English literature should not be understood in anything other than historical, cultural and ethnic terms — as Anglo-Celtic and Judeo-Christian. On the one hand, then, 'the West' is a universal and disinterested category, while on the other it is partial and politicised. Which is it to be? The trick Donnelly doesn't quite pull off is to stop this question from occurring to anyone.

But that's not to say he doesn't try to cosy up to readers by playing the role of the good liberal who cares not only about 'declining standards' in education, but also about declining workplace standards among modern-day educators brought about by bureaucrats obsessed with outcomes-based education (OBE). 'Teachers,' he writes, 'instead of having the freedom to teach [under an OBE system], are overwhelmed with a bureaucratic and intrusive accountability framework where everything has to be measured and ticked off' (35). Elsewhere he refers to the 'unjustified demands' that OBE puts on teachers; no doubt many readers in the secondary education sector would agree and others would as well. What is there to *disagree* with, when bureaucrats are said to be responsible for getting something wrong? When it comes to criticism of the implementation of OBE, indeed, one of us is on record as criticising it strongly, albeit not for the reasons misreported in the press (see Hiatt 2006 and Ferrari 2006). Our objections have to do not with the pedagogy of outcomes-based education as such (on which all we have to say is that 'OBE' is not in-principle synonymous with 'postmodernism'), but with the mishandling of its introduction — in Western Australia at least — by government ministers and education department bureaucrats whose abuses not only of teachers' working conditions, but of their public reputation as a professional class, have met with little resistance from the WA teachers' associations or the unions.

What Donnelly's smug condemnation of 'educrats' and accountability-driven education policy disguises, however, is the fact that the severe cost-cutting to which the education sector and schools (like all public services) have been subjected in recent times, is part and parcel of conservative economic philosophy — regardless of which political party is in government. Admonishing education bureaucrats is as far as Donnelly dares to go, then, in broaching the political economy of OBE or present-day teaching issues. After this, teacher unions and professional associations per se are to be attacked; public money to private schools defended; and under-funding of public schooling ranked behind 'ideology' as an aspect contributing to a decline in education standards:

> Outcomes-based education, along with the imposition of values associated with the cultural-left, have had a profound impact on how curriculum is developed and implemented across Australian schools. The influence of this new-age approach is not restricted to issues like the purpose of education and assessment and reporting, equally as important is the way individual subjects, such as English, history, politics, mathematics and science have been politicised and dumbed down. (72)

Note the abandonment here of previous concerns on behalf of teachers, relating to systemic, bureaucratic problems.

In the end, then, we are left to surmise that the real issue for Donnelly is not that English has become 'postmodern.' The real issue for him has nothing to do with the inequalities and injustices of overworked English teachers, but rather that English studies today is not taught exclusively as Anglo-Celtic/Judeo-Christian studies. The problem, in other words, is not that English in Australia has become 'cultural studies.'

The problem is that it has become the wrong *kind* of cultural studies.

4. Concluding Remarks

Here we speculate: whose interests are served by the war on English, given as we've shown that attacks on postmodernism are without intellectual foundation and cannot be said to further the interests of Leavisim, the Enlightenment or Ancient Greece? So whose interests do they serve?

— Certainly not those of teachers, who appear to us to be overworked, underpaid and publicly vilified. Not only does the war on English *not* address teachers' salaries and working conditions, but it distracts from those issues and other, larger educational issues to do with institutional funding and the like. Such a distraction benefits the economic and other interests of conservatism, for which the straw figures of critical literacy, postmodernism, English teachers and humanities academics are a strategic convenience.

— Indeed the war on English (the attack on postmodernism) *requires* teachers to be 'defective' in order to be 'corrected.' The economic and other interests of conservatism (served no less at present under Rudd than they were under Howard) come together in disciplining teachers' 'wrong-headed,' 'neo-Marxist,' 'feminist,' 'multicultural' distortions of 'the' great works of literature. The war on English creates an 'emergency' requiring government and bureaucratic intervention on behalf of an education system in 'crisis.' But *not* because of the obvious lived crises of teachers and students in regard to overcrowded classes, diminishing administrative support, increased workloads and accountability, and most classroom teachers' inadequate pay.

— Not only for reasons given already, but the war on English does not serve the interests of students. As heirs to the Enlightenment, students of English in Australia today have a right to a contemporary critical training that reflects the latest international developments in the field. This statement would be self-evident if applied to modern-day students of chemistry, say, who are required by society and its education system to undergo contemporary training in chemistry in the context of current international knowledge and practice. But when it comes to English, the development of a critical attitude towards 'absolute' truth and an ability to critically engage with and analyse truth claims in light of best international practice is not seen as a right emanating from the Enlightenment. It's seen as an ideological distortion. (Nor can it be argued that critical literacy or literary theory should be taught only at university level and not in high schools. Who would say this about calculus, for example?) The Enlightenment, however, held a critical attitude to be essential to the capacity of citizens to participate responsibly and democratically in social, cultural and political contexts, through an understanding of their historical and other formations. This, the Enlightenment project, is our inheritance, as ought to be well known to everyone in Australia today — from so-called general readers to so-called newspaper editors alike.

— Such a project, which opponents of contemporary trends in secondary-school English (the editorial staff at the *Australian*, for example, where we would not be surprised to find that Donnelly has a licence to publish even his shopping lists) call 'postmodernism,' serves an *idea* of democracy extending far beyond the mere expression of a political preference at the ballot box. The concept of democracy we have in mind here (see Lucy and Mickler 2006 for further development) is linked inexorably to questions of justice, which always have to do with questions of rights, resources and power. Because the distribution of rights, resources and power remains inequitable, social authorities remain to be questioned — on behalf of an idea of democracy and justice.

As we argue in *The War on Democracy*, the idea and the ideal of democracy can flourish only in an environment of ongoing critical vigilance. The answer to the question, then, of whose interests the war on English serves is this: *whoever is opposed to that environment.*

4. HOW TO WRITE AN ANTI-POMO POTBOILER — THE EXEMPLARY CASE OF GAVIN KITCHING'S *THE TROUBLE WITH THEORY: THE EDUCATIONAL COSTS OF POSTMODERNISM*

1. Be magisterial

This, for example, from the first page of Kitching's preface: postmodernism is 'a very poor, deeply confused and misbegotten philosophy' (Kitching 2008, xi). Note the escalating sweep of the charges and the uncompromising air of self-assurance. Maintain this approach throughout.

2. Keep your key term on the move

When you say 'postmodernism,' you're not obliged to mean what you say. Better yet, why say 'postmodernism' at all when you can say, as Kitching does, 'postmodernism/poststructuralism' (xi), 'postmodernist and poststructuralist ideas' (1), 'poststructuralist and postmodernist political theory' (2), 'poststructuralist or postmodernist theory' (2), 'postmodernist/poststructuralist theory' (3), 'poststructuralist, postmodernist or discourse theory' (5), 'poststructuralism and postmodernism' (8), etc.? Other substitutes include 'intellectually question-begging political radicalism' (xiv), 'philosophical idealism' (39), 'abortive semi-philosophy' (105), 'this extraordinary linguistically determinist world view' (143) and, of course, 'social constructivism' (passim).

By denying that postmodernism has any integrity of its own, you're free to use it as a catch-all for whatever you disapprove of. This makes writing the book a lot easier since it no longer has to be a book about postmodernism as such: it can be a book about stuff that just gets on your goat.

3. Mention a few names, but don't refer to their work

Kitching rarely names names, but when he does they're always used as interchangeable metonyms for a set of core intellectual failings attributed to 'postmodernism' generally and to no one in particular. 'Foucault, Derrida, Laclau and Mouffe,' for example, are of a piece with 'any other luminaries of postmodernism' (xii), making it unnecessary to engage with these figures individually because all postmodernists (or poststructuralists or discourse theorists or social constructivists and so on) think and say the same things. This way you can warn readers against 'following Foucault or Deleuze or Derrida down the paths of deconstruction and social construction of reality' (83), despite none of these three being a social constructivist and only Derrida having really anything to do with deconstruction (a subject you're advised to know nothing about). Because, moreover, all 'postmodernists' are the same and therefore you don't have to account for them individually, you're free to fabricate intellectual genealogies willy-nilly. Just say that the ideas of 'Foucault, Deleuze, etc.' are 'more or less identical' to those of Althusser (85), and blame it all on him.

4. Don't forget rule #1

Say things like: 'I will discuss the real ontological issues' (31) and: 'The problem is this' (31). Or: 'It is time to approach the philosophical heart of matters' (33). Or again: '... now that we have unravelled this particular knot in our thinking' (59).

In the absence of any genuine intellectual authority, just wrap your prose in the rhetorical trappings of authority and you'll be fine. Publishers will love it and the popular press will give you tons of free publicity.

5. Empty your mind of all ideas and let rip your prejudices

The trick here is not simply to make claims but to make outrageous ones, as if you were talking to your neighbour over the back fence. Accuse postmodernism of making people believe that, as Kitching puts it, 'they can be any sex that they want to be' (39)! Then, keeping a straight face, point out that 'some long-term issues of species survival will arise' if men pretending to be women can't 'impregnate' women pretending to be men (39)!

6. Have a favourite philosopher (to whose work you've paid about as much critical attention as the average person gives to reading billboards)

For Kitching it's Austrian-born 'British' philosopher Ludwig Wittgenstein, whom he quotes at one point (more or less at random and almost exclusively from *Philosophical Investigations*) across three-and-a-half uninterrupted pages (48–51) in defiance of the rule that tutors try to instil in first-semester first-years: *Don't let quotations 'speak' for themselves.* 'It does not take much acuity,' Kitching boldly asserts at the conclusion of this pastiche, to understand that Wittgenstein's ideas about language are 'completely different' from those attributed to postmodernism (51), since of course the latter holds to the ludicrous view that linguistic meanings are always multiple and indeterminate. Never mind that you've just quoted Wittgenstein to say there are 'countless different kinds' of language use, and that such 'multiplicity is not something fixed, given once and for all; *but new types of language, new language-games, as we may say, come into existence, and others become obsolete and get forgotten*' (50, Kitching's emphasis).[1] Never mind, too, that this looks suspiciously like an anachronistic affirmation of the postmodern claim that meaning is not a property of language as such, but an effect of contexts and other 'extra'-linguistic (or, more broadly, 'extra'-textual) factors. Never mind either that postmodern über-figure Jean-François Lyotard was greatly influenced by Wittgenstein's notion of language-games, arguing in effect that truth and power are outcomes of rule-dependent moves in a game (see Lyotard 1984, and Lyotard and Thébaud, 1985), or that Wittgenstein's non-representational theory of language is scarcely incompatible with Foucault's understanding of discourses as 'practices obeying certain rules' (Foucault, 1974, 138). Indeed, what might be called the insight of Wittgenstein's later work — that linguistic meanings have no purchase on 'pre-existing' reality — is at least crudely analogous to Foucault's more broadly conceived investigations into the historical developments of certain legal, moral, medical and other codes of practice governing concepts of sexuality, criminality, madness and the like. Foucault's project, then, akin to Wittgenstein's, was speculative and questioning — in a word, genuinely philosophical — rather than systematic or prescriptive, the point being to develop a critical attitude or 'ethos, a philosophical life in which the critique of what we are is at one and the same time the historical analysis of the limits that are imposed on us and an experiment with the possibility of going beyond them' (Foucault, 1984, 50). Never mind any of that, but above all don't worry should it appear that you've quoted your favourite philosopher to the detriment of your own arguments. If you've followed rule #5, you won't have any arguments.

7. Make out that, as a patriarchal elder, you've got pretty much everything sussed

Again, this alleviates the need for arguments and underscores the importance of rule #1. If, like Kitching, you're able to tell your readers that you've been an academic for some thirty years, it will follow that everything you say must be true. Use this authority to give vent to whatever rankles deep inside.

8. Patronise the young

Ridicule the way you think young people talk by writing things (again, after Kitching) like this: 'Wow! Blows you away that thought!' (69), and be sure to condemn the Internet.

9. Bash Foucault

No point trying to deal with all that loopy 'Body without Organs' stuff in Deleuze and Guattari (1983 and 1987) or Derrida (1994) on ghosts, so just get stuck into Foucault! His work at least — seemingly more referential than performative, more 'social sciences' than 'humanities' — appears to be trying to say something about the real world, which (see rule #7) you're an expert on. Make it seem like Foucault thinks we're all imprisoned within 'discourse' (obviously a new-fangled term for 'language'), when in fact Foucault insisted that discourses are both constraining *and* enabling: they enable certain things to count as true at certain times under certain conditions (the modern idea of human rights, for example, relies on a conception of what it means to be human which is neither ahistorical nor, at present, global), and they constrain the limits of what may count as true at any time (humans who qualify as 'fellow citizens' today do so at the exclusion of 'foreigners'). But given that Foucault was interested in the so-called abstract principles, conditions and transformations of a discourse, and not in human consciousness as such, his work is to be rebuked for invoking what Kitching construes as a nightmarishly 'unpeopled world of things' (20), made up only of 'mechanical or inanimate forces' (21). Be careful here not to let on, however, that Foucault himself was all too aware of this way of responding to his work, and indeed pre-empted it by asking the following question:

> What is that fear which makes you reply in terms of consciousness when someone talks to you about a practice, its conditions, its rules, and its historical transformations? What is that fear which makes you seek, beyond all boundaries, ruptures, shifts, and divisions, the great historico-transcendental destiny of the Occident? (Foucault 1974, 209–10)[2]

10. Claim what you're doing as 'evidence-based,' and twist all the evidence in favour of your prejudices

Kitching's evidence takes the form of selected fragments from twenty-seven Honours dissertations (in social and political science) at the University of New South Wales, covering the period 1983–2006. These, he says, all exhibit deep conceptual and rhetorical flaws despite receiving high grades, thus proving (since they are all influenced by 'postmodernism') that postmodernism is flawed! Now for my own part I've read more bad undergraduate essays on *Hamlet* than good ones, but it's never occurred to me to blame this on Shakespeare; so even if Kitching's sample group did reveal some serious intellectual failings, how could this be Althusser's fault? More to the point, it doesn't. By and large the passages Kitching quotes from the dissertations (usually without comment) are well written and informed, as illustrated by the following extract from a thesis taking what appears to be a Foucauldian approach to the issue of refugee detention centres in Australia:

> If the collection of knowledge, data and statistics can determine a power relationship, then the withholding of that knowledge must also have a part to play in unequal power structures and relationships. My argument is that, for example, the very existence of detention centres and the manner in which they are run and presented to the public, limits the amount of knowledge Australian citizens have about detainees. This therefore limits the power that Australian citizens can have in relation to those in detention. Foucault explains this as 'modifying the field of information' which in turn can 'produce effects of power.' (Cited in Kitching 2008, 153)

Note that the trick of presenting data to your own advantage by 'modifying the field of information' is precisely what Kitching performs, as John Frow (2008) has pointed out, by failing to include a control group in his study. There's no way of judging, then, whether the alleged failings of the sample group are peculiarly 'postmodern' or otherwise commonplace. Hence we're told 'there are no "I think"s, "I feel"s, "it seems to me"s etc.' (21) in the sample group, but of course it may simply be that Honours students generally, regardless of being in thrall to postmodernism (or poststructuralism, etc.), lack the self-confidence to write in the first person. Or it may be that a reluctance to use first-person pronouns is a discursive practice of the social and political sciences, with the effect of reinforcing the objectivity of social and political 'scientific' truth. Either way, the lesson here (from Kitching no less than

Foucault) is that the withholding of knowledge is as much an effect of power as the presentation of it.

11. Just when it seems that you couldn't be more patronising, be more patronising

The title of Kitching's penultimate chapter is 'Tips for Teachers and Supervisors' — breathtaking in its presumption and therefore difficult to emulate, but all the same a model to marvel at if not also to aspire to. Here he accuses postmodernism of raising 'a number of profound philosophical issues, issues a teacher in political science, sociology or cultural studies may not even recognise, let alone be equipped to deal with' (130). This from a professor of politics who is not, in any sense that an accredited philosopher would acknowledge, a philosopher! This also from someone who can't read Wittgenstein and doesn't understand postmodernism, who's spent the past fifteen years of his career supervising and examining Honours dissertations on postmodern (or, as Kitching prefers, 'postmodernist') theory without actually having any expertise in the field. Nice work if you can get it, but never mind the contentious professional ethics of this self-posturing: the genre requires you simply to say things like, 'inviting a professional philosopher to act as co-supervisor may not resolve these [profound philosophical] issues' (130). Or: 'one of my aims in writing this book has been to alert my colleagues to these oft-unrecognised philosophical issues in postmodernist theory, and to provide some indication of their depth and difficulty' (130). It's generically imperative, too, that you say this brazenly, even though you haven't cited a single 'postmodern' text beyond the examples from student dissertations collected in your appendix that comprises roughly a quarter of your book.

12. Never underestimate your chances of getting published

Kitching's manuscript was turned into a book. By following the simple rules extracted here, yours could be too.

RUNNING ON

At the 2007 APEC summit in Sydney, where the leaders of nations belonging to the Asia-Pacific economic cooperation forum met, something weird happened. With so many important dignitaries on hand, including the US President and his 650-strong entourage, security in Sydney was understandably tight. A steel-and-concrete barricade stretching for several kilometres along both sides of central city streets marked the borders of a restricted zone extending from the visitors' hotels to the summit venue, forcing local traffic to be re-routed. Sydneysiders were given a public holiday and encouraged to get out of town, presumably to make it all the easier for police and security personnel, armed to the teeth with hi-tech weapons and telecommunications devices, to spot foreign terrorists and stay-at-home domestic troublemakers

---

BORDER LINES. October–December 2007. 'Sure,' I emailed back when John kindly asked me to write this introduction. 'How long … and when do you want it by?' An introduction (from the Latin *intro-* 'inward, to the inside' + *ducere* 'to lead') constitutes 'a leading in.' To the extent that its Latin root is distinguished from the Latin *insinuatus,* meaning to 'bring in by windings and curvings, wind one's way into,' from which we get the English *insinuate,* I take it that an introduction is intended to lead 'inside'

alike. Protest rallies calling for reduced greenhouse gas emissions, or for Australia and the US to pull out of Iraq, were subject to strict state control, and demonstrators with prior convictions were arrested on sight. Shots of security preparations in the city and at Sydney airport, featuring police in riot gear and armoured vehicles fitted with crowd-busting water cannons, were prominent in the national media for days leading up to the summit.

Then, suddenly, in a comedic moment of deconstruction, the unity of all this spectacular apparatus of security (reputedly costing $250 million) was rent asunder. A group of comedians from Australian TV show *The Chaser's War on Everything*, disguised as Canadian APEC officials, drove a motorcade of three black limousines and a motorcycle escort through the fenced-off streets of Sydney's CBD, using false ID cards stamped with 'joke' to clear several checkpoints along the way, before finally being intercepted ten metres outside the entrance to the Intercontinental Hotel where the US contingent was staying. Adding to the already carnivalesque nature of the scene, one of the group (Chas Licciardello) was dressed up to look like Osama bin Laden. He is reported to have stepped from a limousine and said to police, indignantly, 'I am a world leader. Why haven't I been invited to APEC too?'

---

by direct and uncomplicated means. This was probably fine back in Ancient Roman times and earlier, when you were introducing someone, say, to your home, bringing that person — a stranger, presumably — into the place where you lived. But note that even this baseline example requires any inside to have fuzzy borders. Being invited to my home doesn't preclude being asked round for a backyard barbecue and a few beers, in other words, as if this were an invitation to the 'outside' of my home.

Footage of the incident (taken by the comedy show's film crew) was quickly posted on YouTube and televised around the world, no doubt to the amusement of many. But Australian authorities failed to see the funny side and charged the comedians with offences under newly legislated national security laws, which carry a maximum penalty of six months in jail. As Sydney's police chief sternly put it: the group had placed themselves and others in serious danger, because snipers were positioned all over the city and the slightest miscommunication among security forces could have seen things go horribly wrong!

Predictably humourless and admonishing, the response of the police chief and other state officials (along with state advocates, as they might be called, such as conservative media commentators) can be said not to have *read* this event at all. Official representations of the event took it to be saturated with a single meaning that bordered on sedition and justified the state in sanctioning the comedians for having disrespected its authority. Above all, what had to be repelled was any suggestion that the comedians' actions might have exposed the elaborate security measures in Sydney as an inevitably empty and groundless *spectacle* of state control; no more than an *exhibition* of totalising authority manufactured from

---

Still, even allowing for the always already-ness of an inside/ outside problematic — what could it mean to 'bring' someone 'into' a poem or a collection of poems? From welcoming you to my home, or to my hometown or my country and so on, to welcoming you to a book of poems, there is a massive figural leap. If what constitutes the 'inside' of my home is a problem, how much more of a problem would it be to try to decide what constitutes the inside of a book of poetry? Short of the centre

simulacra designed to conceal a lack of presence. How else to account for the consummate ease by which the restricted zone was infiltrated? How else to interpret the event except as farce ... or, more menacingly, as a revelation of just how close civilians might have come, and might always be, to being shot dead by the state in the name of national security if not also (perversely) in the name of democracy?

Nothing undermines the authority of the state, let alone the authority of authority, more so than too much reading. That's why Australian authorities had no choice but to reproach *The Chaser* crew for refusing the solemn univocity of security arrangements at the APEC summit, by reading the meaning and purpose of those arrangements against the interests of the state and demonstrating that their univocity depended on the suppression of other possible interpretations that could be made of them and other possible uses to which they might be put. In this way it is sometimes seditious to crack a joke, even if the joke's effects (as perhaps in the case of *The Chaser* episode) cannot be said to have been consciously intended or fully calculated in advance. A joke, then, can reveal that even the sanctity of a so-called intended meaning is not impervious to ridicule, showing that what anything is said to mean is irreducible to a restricted zone of proper interpretations and

---

pages, what would the inside of a book of poems look like? Or, short of what lies between the covers, what would the inside look like? Clearly, the 'inside' of the poems here, to which I've been invited to 'lead' readers, can't be understood as a material or a spatial centre. I don't think John wanted me to bring you to page, say, 52. Since the 'inside' of a book is not a literal or a physical place, but a metaphysical one and therefore not really a 'place' at all, then in order to refer to what's 'inside'

legitimate truths. The authority of such a zone, together with the authority of a notion of the proper and of the very idea of authority itself, depends on putting all jokes aside.

But by joking here I don't mean (on the contrary) the production of a humorous effect that is necessarily universal, as if it were possible to contemplate a form of comedy that crossed all cultural, national, historical, linguistic and other borders. I mean rather, as we say in Australia, *taking the piss*. To do so is to mock authority, poking fun especially at its self-importance and always — always — with a straight face. You take the piss, in other words, when you create a *pharmakon* effect or a double reading, because for a split second at least the impassive tone and demeanour of your delivery make it undecidable as to whether your intentions are serious or ironic. Piss-taking — as in the case of *The Chaser* crew's simulated performance of a proper APEC group seeming to act in accordance with appropriate rules and procedures, such as those pertaining to the proper image, speed and motion of a cortege — is all about appearing to play by the rules of one language-game while in fact playing by the rules of another. Piss-taking depends on refusing to be interpellated as the obedient subject of a discourse, who would otherwise comply with the expectations of a role assigned to him or her by a

---

Derrida Poems it would be necessary to efface what is literally inside these pages — writing. It's perhaps for this reason that John (as I happen to know) writes poetry on an old manual typewriter, but uses a computer to write prose. Punching those typewriter keys puts him one step closer to an originary act of writing in the sense of having to scratch a surface (the Ancient Greek word *graphein* means 'to write,' as in 'to scratch' a piece of clay with a stylus), which is not to say his poems are somehow

figure, a structure, an institution or some other instance of authority.

The Fool in *King Lear* is an exemplar of the type, but the piss-taker as social critic (in a progressively disruptive, Nietzschean fashion) is perhaps more comfortably aligned, however marginally, with a modernity associated with the Enlightenment. To the extent that the Enlightenment stands for the triumph of *logos* over *mythos*, though, piss-taking is frowned upon by official discourse. The secular, scientistic authority of rational thought (substituting for the theocratic authority of the monarchy and the aristocracy) is intolerant of the dissidence of fools.

Hence the piss-taking prankster is fated to be marginalised from within a metaphysics that takes itself all too seriously. Such a figure at least is destined to be 'controversial,' for daring to confront the Enlightenment with the vanity of its self-importance. Tonally, as it were, the droning seriousness of Kant is deadening to the soul; and for the same reason I can't read Heidegger for long (assuming the jokes haven't been lost in translation) without reaching for my car keys or the remote control. For all that the Enlightenment has given us the possibility of democracy and the promise of a better future to come, for which there is no question that we should

---

therefore more 'authentic' for being written without the aid of digital technology. Since he later transcribes them onto a computer screen, indeed, where he no doubt revises and edits them — re-writes them, as it were, certainly (I have no doubt) in spatial terms — it cannot be said that the poems here were written 'without' the aid of a computer. But regardless of how they were written, their layout evinces a certain quality or attitude that is fated to be lost in quotation. This from

be eternally grateful, sometimes you can't help yourself from wanting the piss to be taken out of everything — concepts, discourses, institutions — that has been reified to an all but mythological level of gravitas commanding nothing but aloof respect.

It is precisely for this reason that deconstruction, for example, which takes the piss out of metaphysics, has never quite been accorded official status by the institution of philosophy (or state philosophy as it might be called, following Deleuze and Guattari); certainly not in the English-speaking West, where the Intercontinental Hotel of authority is re-served more or less exclusively for the delegates of the analytic tradition. The more Derrida wrote, the more his writing caused offence to philosophy's self-representation as a non-metaphorical system in pursuit of transcendental signifieds. Ideally, philosophy goes looking for truths that are already there, waiting to be translated into language; and the more Derrida's writing failed to revere this ideal, by taking the piss out of it, the more his writing came to be dismissed as playfully specious rather than seriously philosophical. The more it came to be seen as a species of poetry, in other words, albeit without it being seen at the same time that all poetry takes the piss out of language.

'Ambition (Sublime)', for example: 'because there's not a word/ in romance languages/adequate, a descriptor of clarity damage,/ heavy trucks on road, the gravel pit/gouged into hillsides.' Strictly this ought to count as a misquotation, insofar as these words are not quite what John *wrote*. They're his words all right — but they're not quite his writing, which relies so much on a use of space. In the poem, each of the lines I've just 'quoted' is located against a background of white emptiness,

Poetry scoffs at the presumption that good sense is a product of plain language use, based on the idea that truth is prior to and independent of its representations. Through unadorned expression, then, *logos* overcomes the dangerous supplementarity of *mythos*. But by extending free passage to others and opening itself to interpretation, every poem mocks the vanity of this presumption that underlies the possibility of a purely referential language; hence the function of the institution of literary criticism is to restrict the in-principle limitless interpretability of poetic texts to a zone of proper meanings, protected by a barricade of mystifying professional-esoteric terminology and knowledge, subject to radical reappraisal from time to time. Taking a different view, what Derrida can be said to have done — every word he wrote — is reducible to this subversive insight: what is true of poetic texts is true of textuality in general. If this were not so — if indeed every text did have an ineluctable core meaning — then someone would have figured out the meaning of *Hamlet* a long time ago, and that would have been that.

Hamlet continues to surprise because it continues to be read in different ways, and not always as an example of literature. In *Specters of Marx*, for instance, Derrida reads it not as an illustration of the pop-psychological consequences

---

which seeps across the book — like the salt lands around York, in Western Australia, perhaps, where John lives, when he isn't living somewhere else, and which he so often writes about. (But before all this 'whiteness' of the book stuff starts sounding all too generically 'poetic,' watch John take the piss out of it in a bathetic simile from 'Echidna': 'the flow of ants as white as Moby Dick'!) The point at any rate is that what can't be quoted here, given the seeming restrictions of the present layout, is the

of procrastination, but for what it has to say politically and philosophically about the spectral nature of democracy-to-come. Such a reading both defies the institutional authority of literary criticism, which values the play for its aesthetic and morally educative qualities, while refusing to respect the proper objects and methods of political philosophy. Derrida reads *Hamlet*, in a word, as text — in excess of its canonical status as a literary masterwork and therefore against the interests of authority vested in established (if not establishment) notions of literature, philosophy and politics.

A disrespect for genre — the mark perhaps of a deconstructive, as distinct from a straightforwardly critical, reading — is a feature too, I think, of John Kinsella's work, extending across poetry, essays, fiction and other kinds of writing. Hilariously — at least to this Australian — one of Kinsella's books is called *Genre* (marketed all too predictably in the publishing world as a novel), a text which defies generic classification while imitating just about every genre under the sun. As a piss-take of the literature department's and the publishing industry's careful attempts to make sense of writing-in-general, by assigning to every text a secure place in the periodic table of writings-in-particular, it is also (as McKenzie Wark notes) part of Kinsella's 'ongoing experiment

---

emptiness 'in' which the lines above are immersed. That emptiness provides not just a context or a background; it *belongs* to those lines. Without it, the lines are incomplete. I can comment on or try to paraphrase the structural necessity of that emptiness, but how could I quote it? Regardless of layout, how would it be possible to 'quote' space? Spacing, then, is an essential feature of John's writing, as it is of writing in general, but it's a feature that has to be overlooked in order to think of

of becoming a writer' (Wark 2000, 256). This experiment — an extravagant essay in border crossing, as it were — is less an act of transgression, requiring the conscious renunciation of a limit, than an affirmation of enjambment. Being John Kinsella is all about running on, spilling over, re-territorialising. Again, as Wark puts it:

> Whether conceived as a hierarchy, from literature to kitsch, or as layered from central to peripheral traditions, writing is one of the most territorialised of the arts. But as the vectors of communication change, so too can the practices of writing and reading. The local can go global without depending on the intermediate step in the hierarchy of aesthetic territories — the nation. But as a paradoxical result, need not renounce the national in order to escape it. (Wark 2000, 271)

Kinsella's status as a national — an 'Australian' — poet is something he neither embraces nor shuns; nor should his 'Australianness' be thought to be translatable into other national contexts, as if the reception to his poetry downunder

---

writing simply as inscriptive 'language' or as written-down speech. Exploiting the inescapably graphic nature of writing (writing and drawing have a common root, from the Greek *graphe*), John turns his poems into works of visual art. Each line is composed of words *and* the space in which those words are suspended, making it difficult to refer to the space 'between' the lines. Visually, one effect of this is to make it seem as if those spaces mark the absence of a former presence,

could be superimposed elsewhere. Lauded overseas for the greatness of his lyric poetry by Harold Bloom and for the greatness of his experimental poetry by Marjorie Perloff, Kinsella's border crossings (and not only between supposedly divergent poetic traditions, as if there were some compelling reason to choose between the Metaphysicals and the Romantics) make him a scandalous figure in the world of Australian letters, where there are those who refer to him dismissively as a big-time operator on the poetry business scene. What most seems to rankle with Australian critics (aside, perhaps, from petty resentment) is that Kinsella so conspicuously *works* at being a poet — through his national and international academic appointments and contacts, his media interviews, his publishing and editorial ventures, his appearances at conferences, festivals and poetry readings — that his poems are tainted with the suggestion of being careerist rather than sincere. 'Somehow,' as Sydney University academic Ivor Indyk wrote, in a now notorious review of Kinsella's *Poems 1980– 1994* for the influential *Australian Book Review*, 'his energy is so overwhelming that it makes the quality of his poetry seem like a secondary consideration' (Indyk 1997). More recently, in a sneering review of Kinsella's *Fast, Loose Beginnings: A Memoir of Intoxications* for the liberal daily, the *Sydney*

---

as if long ago the emptiness had been filled with words. Take the fragment above again, but this time formatted as prose: 'because there's not a word in romance languages adequate, a descriptor of clarity damage, heavy trucks on road, the gravel pit gouged into hillsides.' Re-written 'purely' as language, the fragment barely makes sense at all; reduced to words, it is reduced to a kind of gibberish. Something exceeding a transcription of the purely phonological is going on here, then, which has to do with

Morning Herald, poet and University of Queensland academic Jaya Savige complained that Kinsella 'appears drunk on the éclat of luminous literary acquaintance' while simultaneously (and hypocritically, it is implied) cultivating his status as an outsider (Savige 2006). Further afield, meanwhile, no less a luminous literary authority than Harold Bloom has said of Kinsella that 'if there still be, this late, a "pure" poet, it would be him, free of ideologies and of any histories that are not personal' (Bloom 2003, xxii) — and whatever *that* (in a post-Derridean/Deleuzian/Foucauldian context) might mean, it is clearly intended as praise of an unambiguously high order.

Kinsella's contradictions — he is an Australian who is also a cosmopolitan; an Antipodean *and* a Cambridge poet; a lyricist *and* an experimentalist; a 'pure' poet *and* a publicity seeker; an ex-junkie who is now a vegan; a country boy who knows his way around many of the world's great cities; a critic of the academy who enjoys the institutional and other benefits of professorial residencies at Cambridge and the University of Western Australia, having previously been a Chair at Kenyon College in the United States — loom large in most discussions of his work, fanning the controversy that surrounds both 'it' and the poet 'himself.' The assumption seems to be that the rest of us are fully unified subjects, our innermost selves remaining

---

the visual. You have to *see* the words distributed unevenly on the page to imagine them as remnants of a former unity to which some 'damage' has occurred — an offence beyond words, like a landscape 'gouged' by heavy machinery: an outrage on the imagination. But since this is not a determined effect, what you have to 'see' is also what you have to project. Far from constituting a void, in other words, emptiness, which is writ large in John's poetry but which no writing can

constant around the clock. In compliance with the metaphysics of moderation we consign our becoming to all manner of discursive scrutiny and regulation, as we know from *Discipline and Punish* and other works by Foucault, arresting difference in the bargain. As we know from Derrida, though, a certain idea of writing — as dissemination, as enjambment — takes the piss out of both the sovereign subject and of subjectivity 'itself,' along with the idea that meaning is determined by the elemental properties of a text. Deconstruction goes beyond structuralism, then, both philosophically and in its affrontery (albeit without renouncing structuralism), by dissociating meaning not only from authorial subjectivity, but from the authority of presence in all its conceptual, historical, institutional, political and other forms. Once the signifier–signified relationship is understood as *radically* arbitrary and indeterminate, it is no longer possible to read a text according to the structuralist ideal — as a simultaneous system of internal relations. Simultaneity — the myth of a reading that would describe the operations of the various parts of a text at once, such that the text would be present in its totality — precludes, after all, any consideration of whatever does not conform to it. Whatever 'cannot be spread out into the simultaneity of a form,' as Derrida put it a long time ago, structuralism finds

---

escape is the condition of the possibility of meaning. All authority — philosophical, political and so forth — rests on a refusal of this condition, stubbornly maintaining a resistance to the whiteness of the page or screen. No authority could afford to countenance the possibility that, from the first, all borders are fuzzy; that there is at best only a hazy distinction between a piece of writing and the 'background' on which 'it' is inscribed. What, for instance, is a 'background' that is not *simply* incidental

'intolerable' (Derrida 1978b, 25); and since this is true as well of metaphysics generally, structuralism cannot be confined to a movement or a method associated with the likes of Saussure and Lévi-Strauss. This is why, although structuralists may be good at analysing the formal properties of a joke, it has never occurred to them to crack a few jokes of their own: the metaphysics of authority depends on putting all jokes aside.

Some would say Kinsella was attracted to the *danger* of being attracted to Derrida, consciously or otherwise courting excommunication from the poetry world for associating with a figure who is still more vilified than vindicated in literary circles (outside the academy certainly) worldwide. Others might point even less charitably to Derrida's *notoriety* as the shiny object of Kinsella's desire, re-writing their friendship as a calculated move in the game of managing a reputation for defiance on the poet's part. Within and beyond the academy, such crude psychological speculation remains the order of the day — no less for professional criticism and philosophy than for popular media discourses. After Derrida, then, and after Foucault and Deleuze and Lyotard and Barthes and Baudrillard and all the rest, the motorcade of metaphysics continues to run its course, those seeking to disrupt it having been overcome for now by the official and unofficial security

---

marginal, external or supplementary? Against such a background, what would there 'be' to foreground? These are not just 'philosophical' questions either, which might be said to draw their force from Derrida's work. They are also *Australian* questions, which I think is why John finds Derrida's work so fascinating. 'Australia,' in a sense, is *all* background to European eyes — not only an empty, featureless landscape, but also a cultural desert from the perspective of Europe as the cultural

forces of a new world order of seriousness in the face of imminent terrorist attacks. In this context, nothing serves the interests of metaphysics — let alone the West's interest in oil — better than a prosaic imagination.

That's what I think the poems in this collection are 'about,' although not in any kind of thematic sense. What I think attracts Kinsella to Derrida's writing is not so much the shock value (though of course he is aware of this effect) as the *mundanity* of deconstruction, which takes a certain kind of imagination — a poetic or aesthetic imagination — to respond to without fear or favour, or without prejudice of a certain kind. How could a statement such as Derrida's now notorious claim in the *Grammatology*, that 'there is nothing outside of the text' (158), be read by a poet, except as a perfectly unextraordinary thing to think or say — despite many real-life poets' denial that Derrida wrote anything worth reading at all? What does it tell us about the world and what it may be necessary to change, when the positions of soft-hearted liberals and hard-line conservatives alike are as one in condemning deconstruction for disrespecting the authority of tradition, Western values and standards of truth? When liberals *and* conservatives are arm-in-arm opposed to the dangerous 'relativism' of deconstruction, what does this tell us about deconstruction?

---

centre. We're just the 'telegraphic band' bit of Derrida's 'Living On/Border Lines' (175), the footnote that isn't quite a footnote, running along beneath the main body of the text, turning every part of that expression, 'beneath the main body of the text,' into a problem. From black swans to egg-laying mammals, difference is the norm downunder; and since everything belonging to the history of metaphysics was decided on in the certain knowledge that all swans are white, we are both surplus

One of the ways in which the poems here can be seen to respond to such a question is simply by taking that question seriously, which is to say by taking deconstruction seriously. Which is to say, by not taking deconstruction *too* seriously. Take the following fragment from 'The Echidna and Hedgehog Bear Only Superficial Resemblances':

> birdsnoutducklike
> all mammary glands
> and egg drop
> and body hair
> mammal inter reptilian
> but not a metamorphosis,
> which is so convenient
> for the human condition,
> as lucrative as television

This is not what the writing of a professional philosopher, a sociologist or a literary critic looks like, though it does tolerate a certain similarity to the writing of my ten-year-old son. Children write 'poetically,' in other words, before they learn how to write prose. They assemble words haphazardly, 'creatively,' on a page or screen, seemingly unencumbered by the need to stretch

to the requirements of an idea of the West *and* an affront to metaphysics. When, for example, the natural is understood in terms of verdant fields and rolling pastures, then this land of 'wry vegetation' (as John calls it in 'Echidna Photomontage'), which exceeds the imagination of the science of botany, must threaten the very concept of nature itself. But if the authority of universal truth came unstuck when *The Endeavour* landed at Botany Bay (at around the time Kant was writing *The*

each line of type or script to fit a standard margin width. They create, or simply form, weird new 'words' out of combinations of existing words and syllables — *birdsnoutducklike* — long before learning to recognise these as portmanteau words, like 'actuvirtuality' or 'phonocentrism.' They describe things elliptically, and almost exclusively through a mixture of parataxis, conjunction and enjambment: 'all mammary glands/ and egg drop/and body hair/mammal inter reptilian.' In this way poetry — or the creative force of children's language use — is precisely what has to be unlearned in order to learn to write prose. Prose (when it isn't fiction) is poetry stripped of its creative force, and we learn to write it acceptably only by forgetting that, before we learned to write 'properly,' we played with language in the absence of any pressure to conform to the referential imperative of professional non-fiction, as if writing on the basis of a mundane truth: *there is nothing outside of the text.* Between poetry and prose, then, there are only superficial resemblances, though we are said to write prose well (rather than just adequately) by virtue of a certain metamorphosis with poetry, whenever our writing incorporates a trope, a striking turn of phrase or some other prosodic feature deployed to good effect. Poetic devices, but not quite poetry as such, can lead therefore to lucrative professional and cultural, if not also

---

Critique of Judgement), it has not resulted in an affirmation of the Enlightenment adage — 'dare to know' (Kant 1970, 54). Downunder, differences have tended to be repressed rather than affirmed. Far from recognising the sovereignty of Aboriginal people, then, successive Australian governments have sought to assimilate them into modernity — even at the expense of taking away their children and placing them in the care of church and state institutions, where they've been exposed to sexual and

financial, rewards, for those judged to control their otherwise chaotic — pre-prosaic — potential.

This is what Wark means when he calls writing one of the most territorialised of the arts. So we have poets, and we give them a licence to write 'poetically' or aesthetically (according to a certain idea of literature), relegating poetry to a 'special' kind of writing and in the process delimiting what it can be used to do. And so we have critics, and we give them the authority not only to determine what counts as poetry but also to police its borders. And so we have institutions, and we give them the authority to sanction and patrol the limits of what counts as poetry. And so we have a publishing industry, and we give it the authority to market poetry to readers. In all of this what we don't have is an idea of writing in general ... and so we have philosophers, and we give them the authority to be philosophical by virtue of showing us the extent of their mastery over the irruptive, aleatory, figural and other undesirable effects of language. Which is to say, of poetry. And so we have historians, and we give them the authority to tell us what history means ... and so on.

Poetry comes before prose, which is what this territorialising system is designed to suppress. And because poetry comes before prose, Derrida sometimes delighted in taking the piss

---

other forms of abuse. Like the attempted translation of our 'wry vegetation' into patches of cultivated lawn, the attempted translation of our Indigenous fellow citizens (to whom citizenship was denied until little more than thirty years ago) into modern state subjects is based on the assumption that their difference constitutes a deficiency in need of correction. Such is the inevitable violence of every attempt to translate a poem into prose. It's in this context that I think John may well regard

out of the idea of a well-formatted page (as the image of a well-formulated argument). Think, for instance, of *Dissemination* and *Glas*, which are in a sense indebted to the later Heidegger while at the same time taking the piss out of his views on the poetic 'essence' of language by showing that what is proper or primordial to language, what is 'essential' to it, cannot be understood in positive terms. Errancy — writing's unconscious, as it were — doesn't just come into play when language is used inappropriately or carelessly, but is rather a condition of linguistic and textual usage in general. 'Honest' — that's what Kinsella calls (in the final poem here, 'Heidegger and Poetry (*Istrice* 2)') 'the route of the errant,' which cannot be taken en masse. Errancy and honesty are always singular, in other words, never arising from a *system* — of reading or living — which could substitute for a responsibility to make decisions in the absence of a rule of judgement. So in the 'poetic' episodes of some of his work, where Derrida's writing is conspicuous in quite literal ways (as if in reaction to the po-faced seriousness of the *Grammatology*), his textual inventiveness or playfulness isn't simply 'textual.' It is also 'honest,' in a non-prescriptive, asystematic, quasi-unethical sense, according to which the ethical will have begun — as will the poetic — only when *The* work of interpretation happens, which cannot happen when

---

Derrida's *Dissemination* and *Of Grammatology* (among his other works) as the best histories ever to be written of Australia, despite being written by someone who spent no more than a few days in this country (in Sydney, where he delivered two public seminars in August 1999: see Patton and Smith, 2001) not long before he died. What Derrida's work could be said to offer John is an understanding or affirmation that the only appropriate way of responding to difference is by seeking to do the least

the limits of interpretability or of what is meant by 'reading' are predetermined by an institution or some other system or structure of authority. 'One must behave not only,' as Derrida remarks in *The Gift of Death*, 'in an ethical or responsible manner, but in a nonethical, nonresponsible manner, and one must do that *in the name of* duty, of an infinite duty, *in the name of* absolute duty' (Derrida 1995a, 67).

In what might be called the 'poethical' episodes of some of his work, then, Derrida's writing calls to be engaged with from outside the constraints of standard sense-making protocols. This — turning readers into active participants in the production of meanings by opening the possibility of doing philosophy differently and doing different things with it — raised the ire of straitlaced philosophers, who could not but look on any disruption to the solidified territorialisation of writing as a professional threat. Their ungracious indignation stooped to its lowest point in the early 1990s, when some Cambridge dons (including a few from Kinsella's own Churchill College, though this was before his time there) tried to block Cambridge's offer of an honourary doctorate to Derrida for services to philosophy (see Lucy 1995 for the details). Deconstruction it seemed was no laughing matter, and the best way of putting a stop to its profanities was to

---

possible violence. This is to recognise that as every patch of lawn downunder represents the trace of a violent encounter with the natural habitat, which is seen as monstrous and therefore 'unnatural' according to the metaphysics of presence, so too is the history of our treatment of Aboriginal people underwritten by a certain abhorrence of others. For all that the Enlightenment dared to know, it was not fond of fuzzy borders (which is no doubt why it took so long for the Third Critique to be taken

try to have Derrida, in effect, deregistered! And so now all these years later another Cambridge don — albeit from the antipodes, at the limits of Western civilisation — has written a book of poems, in effect, 'for' Derrida, if not quite about him. In the context of what ought to be Cambridge's shame, the ethics of this gesture should not go unnoticed.

Where others rail, Kinsella simply accepts — that is the nature of the ethical here. Such acceptance is both personal *and* poetic (so that perhaps Kinsella is indeed a 'pure' poet after all, but for reasons having nothing to do with the fantasy of his absolute independence from history and ideology), inasmuch as poetry is the most accepting of all forms of writing in the most general sense. The key to poetry's textuality is that it doesn't have a key, the rules of a poem's composition remaining always something of a mystery compared to other literary and certainly most non-literary works. Kant knew this — or at least the Kant of the Third Critique did, in regards to a certain idea of art or the aesthetic, which he took to be whatever posed the principles of its formation as a *question* to which there could be no universal response. What Derrida did — his move — was to extend Kant's move beyond the borders of art or poetry ... to textuality in general. Hence the beginning of 'Plato's Pharmacy', in *Dissemination*, which a 'pure' poet like Kinsella

---

seriously as a work of philosophy); and there's nothing fuzzier than the *idea* of someone who doesn't look like you, which is no doubt why for so long Aboriginal people were officially classified as part of this country's flora and fauna — literally, as other than human. So much depends, we might therefore insist, on the deconstruction of the unity of a piece of writing, which could be the lesson that John draws from Derrida — and which Derrida himself came close to acknowledging that he drew from a

could scarcely help himself from quoting here: 'A text is not a text unless it hides from the first comer, from the first glance, the law of its composition and the rules of its game' (Derrida 1981, 63). Understood as a radical affirmation of the desire of textuality to be free, the effects of this affirmation — and deconstruction, as John D. Caputo tells us, *is* this affirmation (Caputo 1997, 97–8) — cannot be confined to a restricted zone of the aesthetic. So, for example, before *The Chaser* episode at the APEC summit in Sydney is satirical, political or seditious — it is textual.

Or — every reading is an attempt to translate a poem into prose.

No matter how finely attenuated or carefully sensitive the reading, what must escape this process is the poem's singularity. Its difference. In attempting to translate the unpresentable into words, however, not even poems can avoid bringing about this loss, regardless of the service they might be said to perform in heightening our awareness of difference — of differences — in the first place. The echidna is different from the hedgehog, after all, and its Australianness resists translation into the languages of Europeans, except as a kind of curiosity — a freak of nature — that helps to define what 'Australia' means to others. In its very name, given to the mother of all monsters in Greek

---

certain idea of what is called 'literary' writing as exemplified by poetry: 'Perhaps,' he once said, 'all I wanted to do was to confide or confirm my taste (probably unconditional) for literature' (Derrida 1995b, 27). A certain relation to poetry, then, while indeterminate, is also indispensable to an understanding of Derrida's writing, helping to explain why so many philosophers don't 'get' it — and why John does. John's got no problem, for example, with the *pharmakon* effect of modernity, which

mythology, the echidna is marked as a zoological outrage — a mammal that lays eggs! — from within the metaphysics of the natural sciences, which the poems here reveal as Eurocentric. Seeming to morph reptile and mammal ('depositing eggs/ and suckling progeny/on milk,' Kinsella writes in 'Amnesty Echidna Manifesto'), this impossible Australian creature with a European name is 'monstrous' only for taking the piss out of a certain taxonomy of living things. In outward appearance the echidna resembles the creature that is called the *hérisson* in French and, in Italian, the *istrice*: a small animal covered in spiky quills, which the English call a hedgehog. So the echidna's 'monstrosity' lies in its *difference* from the European 'original'; a difference that isn't scientific but cultural through and through, condemning the echidna to play the role of the *hérisson*'s other within a system that is European through and through. From the echidna's point of view, it's the *hérisson* that is the monster — a mammal that can't lay eggs! But of course there is no room in metaphysics for an antipodean perspective, since truth is not 'perspectival' (think of Nietzsche's place — downunder — in the taxonomy of philosophical seriousness). No room for different 'takes' on whatever metaphysics deems to be so; no room for differences at all. When it's *your* culture that has the authority to determine the order of things — the way things are — why

---

he accepts as both the cause and the cure of drought in the Australian bush. ('If cured of its thirst,' he writes in 'Prologue', the salmon gum would still 'retain/its addiction.') Nor does he have a problem — far from it — with the 'echidna effect' of the Australian landscape, where so many of the plants and animals (together with the 'alien' appearance of the terrain and the light) seem monstrous, but which for John are no less beautiful and compelling for seeming so. 'This is not' (as he puts it in 'Fourth

would you compromise that authority by entertaining the influence of 'alternative' points of view? Far from conceding or even acknowledging that such alternatives had any authority at all, wouldn't you be more inclined to denounce them from the position of a linguistic, philosophical, institutional, economic, political — and, if needs be, military — authority that was yours to wield?

Such is the condition of global politics as defined by the hegemony of the West ... yet who would have thought a few poems to have so much blood in them? Then again, perhaps, Kinsella may have chosen to write about the echidna for personal reasons linked to his friendship with Derrida, who, as we know from *Fast, Loose Beginnings* (Kinsella 2006, 174–85), was fascinated with echidnas — the trace of an old world response to the shock of the new? — and often spoke about them with Kinsella. Since he is unlikely to have done so with many others, the echidna may figure in these poems as a mark of something that was unique to Derrida's relationship with Kinsella and which the poet may therefore cherish. But I'd prefer to leave this to the biographers and literary critics to decide.

The question is not what the echidna means, but what we can do with it. What, for example, does it allow us to think?

Essay on Linguistic Disobedience') 'romanticism' ... as if it were possible to get outside of modernity in order to critique it — or, even more fancifully, to reject it. For John, as for Derrida, there's no going back. Which is not to say there is a *determined* way of going forward. To know this is to accept responsibility for whatever might happen next, without allowing things to happen on the basis that their meanings must be preordained. So instead of thinking of the future as a prosaic continuation of the past, we

To ask this question is to see that the *text* of the echidna — and the echidna is textual before it is scientific — is not bound by the context of this collection, since context is never singular. There is no outside of context, in a word, and this opens the echidnas in these poems to a multiplicity of points of view, possible uses and contingent associations and effects. Kinsella mines these for all they're worth. The seemingly misshapen layout of 'Odour', for instance, appears abnormal or eccentric only when judged against a standard expectation of what a poem should look like, a standard which is not antipodean but European. The poem is not so much bent *out* of shape, then, by comparison to a European poetic ideal, as bent *into* it in sympathy with its environment — for in its seeming irregularity the poem might be said to pattern itself after the meanderings of its referent:

> here or there
> we might enter the territory —
> nothing personal
> though an echidna
> curled up
> by a jamtree
> elicits
> a genetically imprinted reaction:

ought to be thinking of it as a poem — open to interpretation. Open, precisely because what every poem (and every projected future) 'lacks' is an inviolable unity protected by the security of stable borders, separating poetry, say, from philosophical and other kinds of writing ... or the future from *any* relation to a past. What, in other words, could count as the a priori apparatus by which it would be possible to determine one 'unity' from another: imagination, for example, from reason?

> hey,
>   take a whiff of this!
>   they named this place
>   after your grandfather,
>   and recorded his mark
>   on the map; hey, note
>   the bush's timbre —

As an Australian, I can't read these lines without thinking of the ways by which the first people of this country map and name the land with reference to ancestral lineages. As a non-Indigenous Australian, though, I can't claim to understand these other ways of reading and writing the country, which mark Aboriginal people as 'spiritual' and therefore as non-scientific and pre-modern. Indigenous difference, too, human indigenous difference, is the other of the *hérisson* or the hedgehog, helping to explain the appalling third world conditions under which most Aboriginal people live in Australia today, as citizens of a first world democracy. 'The drive to the pharmacy/is long in the country,' Kinsella writes in 'Prologue', and indeed it is — for Aborignal people living on outback communities seeking recompense for the abuses of Europeans who dispossessed them of their land ... and who also need the cars to get them

---

What could keep them from running on? Or by what predetermined, hard and fast rule could the 'proper' section of this text be separated from (as it were) the 'antipodean' section; a text that was written, in defiance of a certain notion of unity, across several months and in several cities — from Fremantle in Western Australia, where I live, to Prague, Rome and Sydney, where I've been conferencing and holidaying of late? What kind of 'unity' could derive from having

there. Small wonder, then, that one of the poems here is called 'Echidna Democratic', especially in the recent context of Australian security forces being granted extraordinary powers of governance (at the state's behest) over the local affairs of many Aboriginal people in remote parts of the nation still awaiting the arrival of modernity.

Reading is not decoding, in other words. It's all about — in deconstructive and poetic ways, in radical and mundane ways — not quite falling into the trap of thinking that meaning is an effect of genre, which is perhaps why so many of the poems in this collection are made up of a mixture of genres, but without therefore becoming 'hybrids,' in defiance of the law that genres are not to be mixed! The poems here run on, then, not simply in a technical sense, but in full submission to the enervating force of writing, of textuality in general, 'without which,' as Derrida put it, 'language would not be what it is' (Derrida 1978b, 27). It is precisely this force (which Derrida sometimes called *dissemination* or *differance*) that every form of critical commentary on a text must overlook, in order to produce the myth of a total reading. And it's precisely this myth that Kinsella's poems delight in taking the piss out of. Or as someone puts it in 'Fourth Essay on Linguistic Disobedience':

---

crossed so many borders? That's the question, I think, which these poems insinuate, and the answer is not: *no unity at all.* But what I think these poems help to engender is an understanding that every 'unity' — in the form of a poem or a nation, say — constitutes a violation of differences. (The wandoo may not be an oak, but that doesn't mean it's not a tree; the hedgehog may not lay eggs but that doesn't mean it's not a mammal.) Accepting this is not to be

> Belonging to this is not desirable.
> Unbelonging, I make conversation
> with like-minded people. A wedge-tailed eagle is
> seen
> on a fence-post and none of the party wants to
> shoot it. I select
> this society.

Linguistic disobedience for Kinsella, I suspect, is civil disobedience which I think for him is what poetry means. And pure poets have a responsibility to dress up as Osama bin Laden and say, 'I select this society.'

---

committed to rejecting authority, but to taking the piss out of it. By dressing up as Osama bin Laden ... or writing a poem.

CODA: AUSTRALIAN CASTLES

Following its overwhelming electoral victory in 1996, the Keating Labor Government announced its bold plan for cultural revolution. Everything hinged on the *Australian Castles* project, initiated the following year.

By Christmas 1999, Australia had its first castle — Balmoral, in Bendigo — chosen by the PM for maximum symbolic impact. As a lesson in appropriation, the Bendigo Balmoral showed up the Scottish Balmoral for the simulacrum that it was.

Originally a sixteenth-century tower house, Balmoral Castle in Scotland was built in 1855 as a gift from Prince Albert to Queen Victoria. Keating knew that Albert was attracted to the tower house because the surrounding woodlands reminded him of Thuringia in his native Germany, and so Keating saw Balmoral as a perfect illustration of what he took to be true of British history in general — there was nothing terribly 'historical' about it. British history, he understood, was all about appropriation, imitation and symbolic inventiveness. Since these were not the exclusive property of any nation, Keating saw the Bendigo 'copy' as an opportunity to expose the Victorian 'original' for the imitation it had always been.

From this lesson a cultural revolution was born.

The 'new' Victorian Balmoral was an immediate success, drawing thousands of visitors a day. Cardiff Castle in Wales, which Keating commissioned for Canberra — reasoning that someone's idea of an enchanted fairytale castle built in the nineteenth century on the remains of a Roman fort would make a perfect image for the seat of government — also proved to be hugely popular, as did the ruins of Fremantle's Penmark Castle from thirteenth-century Glamorgan.

Today there are hundreds of Australian castles, pillars of a nation without nationalism. But only half a century ago our history as a footnote to Europe oppressed us.

Keating's Lesson led straight to radical reform, especially the *Welcome, Stranger* immigration policy of 2001. As every Australian schoolchild now knows, the lesson was that history has always been postmodern. The past has no essence, no unifying spirit ... and cannot determine our identity.

NOTES

INTRODUCTION

1. This is an admittedly difficult conception of democracy, but nevertheless crucial to my concerns here. At the risk of offending shock jocks and op. ed. writers for not striking a familiar tone, let me say that the issue has to do with an affirmation of democracy as the radical *promise* of a better future to come that can never be realised. That promise is irreducible to democracy understood as a system of representative government that may or may not lead to social reform, though of course it does not preclude this familiar understanding. As Derrida puts it — in language suited to an idea that isn't plain — the essence of democracy is that 'not only will it remain indefinitely perfectible, hence always insufficient and future, but belonging to the time of the promise, it will always remain, in each of its future times, to come: even when there is democracy, it never exists, it is never present, it remains the theme of a non-presentable concept' (Derrida 1997, 306).

1. TABLOID DECONSTRUCTION

1. Bill Henson is an Australian photographic artist whose work is held in major collections in Australia, Europe and the United States. His Paddington exhibition scandalised not only Devine but also, among others, Prime Minister Kevin Rudd, who publicly denounced Henson's work as 'revolting.' In the immediate wake of the scandal caused by Devine's article earlier in the day, the opening of the exhibition was postponed to the following evening (23 May 2008) and many of Henson's pieces were temporarily seized by New South Wales police with a view to charges being laid against both the artist and the gallery owner under the Crimes Act. In June, however, police decided not to prosecute after receiving advice that Henson's images had been given a PG rating by the Office of Film and Literature Classification and were suitable for viewing by children under the age of 16 if accompanied by a parent or guardian.

2. The Platonic preference — underpinning, Derrida contends, the history of Western philosophy — for spoken over written truth derives from the *Phaedrus*, in which Plato maintains that the presence of the speaker guarantees the truth of what is said, whereas the absence of the writer opens writing to the risk of misinterpretation. Briefly, Derrida's intervention in this history, which grounds truth in 'presence,' takes the form of arguing (in *Of Grammatology* and elsewhere) that presence is not quite the opposite of absence, and therefore isn't quite a ground at all. The presence of a speaker, for example, is no guarantee that he or she will speak the truth or that his or her words won't be misinterpreted; nor does it guarantee that what he or she might intend to say will in fact be what is said, or that he or she will *only* say what is intended, and so on. Speech, then, no less than writing, is subject to errancy, indeterminacy and misinterpretation, and therefore presence is not quite the opposite of absence and can't be thought to ground truth. For Derrida on the speech–writing opposition see Lucy 2004, 118–30.

3. An allusion might be drawn here to Plato's reference (in the *Phaedrus*) to the *pharmakon* of writing, where the Greek work is translated usually either as 'poison' or 'cure': either the technology of writing 'poisons' the purity of so-called natural speech, by enabling what was said to be transmitted in the absence of the speaker (who is no longer present to vouch for his or her intentions), or it 'cures' speech of being prone to be forgotten. But *pharmakon* has many other possible meanings: 'illness,' 'drug,' 'substance,' 'charm,' 'remedy,' 'spell,' 'medicine' and more. Even within its original language, then, and before becoming a problem simply of 'translation,' *pharmakon* harbours its opposite (drug–medicine, illness–remedy, substance–spell, etc.) within 'itself.' Derrida's point in *Dissemination* is that the word *pharmakon* is so overdetermined, so replete with signification, that it can't quite be said to 'signify' at all; at any rate it can't be said to signify in the standard sense of referring to something clear and unambiguously 'outside' itself, in the sense required by 'plain language' (as espoused by philosophy, for example, but these days no less by talk-back radio and the popular press — a point of convergence that philosophy hasn't shown much interest in wanting to confront) for distinctions to be drawn and maintained (see Derrida 1981). Right at the origin — Plato's *Phaedrus* — the differences between 'speech' and 'writing' are far from clear and distinct; indeed, they 'mimic' the negative properties that Plato ascribes to the 'new' technology

of writing, and in this sense (albeit one that isn't common) writing can be said to come *before* speech. All the 'unwanted' properties associated with writing — overdetermination, errancy, fallibility, indeterminacy, ambiguity and so forth — are there already 'in' language, as exemplified by the *pharmakon*. So the kind of distinction that is necessary to sustain an opposition between speech and writing, or to sustain oppositional structures in general, requires the suppression of an otherwise irrepressible force within language (or, more generally, textuality) that causes meanings to spill across, run on and overlap rather than conform to fixed and stable categories. In short, the speech–writing opposition doesn't hold.

4. See the website, *The Unthrown Kids*: <http://www.safecom.org.au/kids-overboard.htm>.

5. The Pope's visit was occasioned by World Youth Day, which saw nearly a quarter of a million 'pilgrims' from 170 nations descend on Sydney from 15 to 20 July 2008.

2. EVERYBODY LOVES RAYMOND WILLIAMS

1. See Lucy and Mickler (2006), especially Chapter 1 ('Luke Slattery and Knowledge', 11–28); and Chapter 3 in the present volume.

2. Despite the inference that 'critical literacy' and 'postmodernism' are not the same, the negative features Turner ascribes to the former are typical of those ascribed by others (see Chapters 3 and 4) to the latter. While of course I think that 'postmodernism' often appears as a misnomer, the point is that Turner's use of 'critical literacy' conveys many of the features attributed (with varying degrees of felicity) to 'postmodernism' elsewhere. If it looks like a duck and it walks like a duck ...

3. 'Bricolage,' in effect, is French for 'DIY.' Lévi-Strauss uses it to refer to the nature of mythological discourse, which he argues is put together contingently from symbols and personal (or group) experiences that are to hand, in contrast to scientific discourse, which is understood as impersonal and entirely referential. Derrida's point is that this seemingly neat distinction between the unruly and the systematic (such that scientific discourse assumes the status of a pure independent method in search of pre-existing truth) is itself a myth, because the necessity to borrow ideas, formulae, concepts, methods,

styles and other materials from 'the text of a heritage which is more or less coherent or ruined' turns all discourse into bricolage (Derrida 1978a, 285).

4. On Slattery's views in the *Australian*, see Lucy and Mickler (2006, 11–28); for responses, see Slattery (2007a, 2007b). For a discussion of Donnelly's views, see the following chapter.

5. Kalbarri is an isolated fishing town several hours north of Perth. Kirribilli is a small exclusive suburb in the 'wealth belt' of Sydney's North Shore.

6. See Stuart Macintyre's review (2007) of Donnelly's book, and for further discussion see Chapter 3.

3. THE WAR ON ENGLISH

1. Far from being liberal humanist in the sense Donnelly appears to mean, the Greeks practised an 'aesthetics of existence,' as Foucault calls it, referring to 'a way of life whose moral value did not depend either on one's being in conformity with a code of behaviour, or on an effort of purification' (Foucault 1990, 89).

2. See Lucy and Mickler (2006) for a development of this point.

3. See Lucy and Mickler (2009) for a development of the argument that a certain version of the left is no less self-interestedly against 'postmodernism' than the right.

4. Hence the essay's extended title, *A Modest Proposal For Preventing the Children of Poor People in Ireland From Being Aburden to Their Parents or Country, and For Making Them Beneficial to The Public.*

5. See Lucy (1997) *Postmodern Literary Theory: an Introduction,* for further discussion on this, especially in regards to a 'tradition' of romanticism.

6. Donnelly gives the reference as a letter entitled 'The Priestly Travesty' in John Tasker's *F.R. Leavis Letters in Criticism.* In fact Tasker is the editor (and not the author) of a collection of Leavis's published letters, entitled simply *Letters in Criticism.* The letter to which Donnelly refers appeared originally in *The New Statesman* for 8 December 1956.

7. Donnelly's reference credits Patai and Corral as the authors of a book entitled simply *Theory's Empire.* In fact they are the editors of this book, the subtitle of which is *An Anthology of Dissent.*

4. HOW TO WRITE AN ANTI-POMO POTBOILER

1. The passage contains a minor misquotation: Kitching's 'once and for all' appears in *Philosophical Investigations* simply as 'once for all' (Wittgenstein 1953, §23).

2. The question could be put to Kevin Donnelly (2007) as well, albeit for him the Occident is more or less exclusively Anglo-Celtic (see Chapter 3).

REFERENCES

Arnold, Matthew (1969) *Culture and Anarchy*. London: Cambridge University Press.

Auty, Giles (2000) 'Postmodernism's Assault on Western Culture', *Quadrant*. June: <http://members.optushome.com.au/jimball/Postmodernism.html>.

Barthes, Roland (1982) *Camera Lucida: Reflections on Photography*, trans. Richard Howard. New York: Hill and Wang.

Bloom, Harold (2003) 'Introduction' in John Kinsella, *Peripheral Light: Selected New Poems*. Fremantle: Fremantle Arts Centre Press, xiii–xxviii.

Caputo, John D. (1997) *The Prayers and Tears of Jacques Derrida: Religion Without Religion*. Bloomington: Indiana University Press.

Deleuze, Gilles and Félix Guattari (1987) *A Thousand Plateaus: Capitalism and Schizophrenia*, trans. Brian Massumi. Minneapolis: University of Minnesota Press.

Deleuze, Gilles and Félix Guattari (1983) *Anti-Oedipus: Capitalism and Schizophrenia*, trans. Robert Hurley, Mark Seem and Helen R. Lane. Minneapolis: University of Minnesota Press.

Department of Education, Tasmania, *English Learning Area*: <http://wwwfp.education.tas.gov.au/English/critlit.htm>.

Derrida, Jacques (1997) *The Politics of Friendship*, trans. George Collins. London: Verso.

Derrida, Jacques (1995a) *The Gift of Death*, trans. David Wills. Chicago: University of Chicago Press.

Derrida, Jacques (1995b) 'Passions: "An Oblique Offering"', trans. David Wood, in *On the Name*, ed. Thomas Dutoit. Stanford: Stanford University Press, 3–31.

Derrida, Jacques (1994) *Specters of Marx: The State of the Debt, The Work of Mourning and The New International*, trans. Peggy Kamuf. New York: Routledge.

Derrida, Jacques (1990) *Glas*, trans. John P. Leavy Jr and Richard Rand. Lincoln: University of Nebraska Press.

Derrida, Jacques (1985) 'Racism's Last Word', trans. Peggy Kamuf, *Critical Inquiry* 12: 290–9.

Derrida, Jacques (1981) *Dissemination*, trans. Barbara Johnson. Chicago: University of Chicago Press.

Derrida, Jacques (1979) 'Living On/Border Lines' in *Deconstruction and Criticism*, eds Harold Bloom et al. London: Routledge & Kegan Paul, 75–176.

Derrida, Jacques (1978a) 'Structure, Sign, and Play in the Discourse of the Human Sciences' in *Writing and Difference*, trans. Alan Bass. London: Routledge & Kegan Paul, 278–93.

Derrida, Jacques (1978b) 'Force and Signification' in *Writing and Difference*, trans. Alan Bass. London: Routledge & Kegan Paul, 3–30.

Derrida, Jacques (1976) *Of Grammatology*, trans. Gayatri Chakravorty Spivak. Baltimore: Johns Hopkins University Press.

Devine, Miranda (2008a) 'Moral Backlash Over Sexing Up of Our Children', *The Sydney Morning Herald*, 22 May: <http://www.smh.com.au/news/opinion/moral-backlash-over-sexing-up-of-our-children/2008/05/21/1211182891875.html>.

Devine, Miranda (2008b) 'Artistic Crowd the Real Philistines', *The Sydney Morning Herald*, 29 May: <http://www.smh.com.au/news/miranda-devine/puerile-defence-of-henson/2008/05/28/1211654120223.html>.

Devine, Miranda (2004) 'Riding the Conservative Revolution', *The Sydney Morning Herald*, 14 October: <http://www.smh.com.au/articles/2004/10/13/1097607297531.html>.

Donnelly, Kevin (2007) *Dumbing Down: Outcomes-based and Politically Correct — The Impact of the Culture Wars on Our Schools*. Prahran: Hardie Grant.

Ferrari, Justine (2006) 'Curriculum Changes "Lowering Standards"', *The Australian*, 3 April: 3.

Foucault, Michel (1990) *The History of Sexuality*, Vol. 1: *The Use of Pleasure*, trans. Robert Hurley. New York: Vintage.

Foucault, Michel (1984) 'What is Enlightenment?', trans. Catherine Porter in *The Foucault Reader*, ed. Paul Rabinow. New York: Pantheon, 32–50.

Foucault, Michel (1974) *The Archaeology of Knowledge*, trans. A.M. Sheridan Smith. London: Tavistock.

Frow, John (2008) '[Review of] Gavin Kitching, *The Trouble with Theory*', *Australian Literary Review*, 13 August: 5, 6.

Hamilton, Clive (2006) 'Churches Could Hold Key to Salvation for the Left', *Eureka Street*, 26 December: <http://www.eurekastreet.com.au/article.aspx?aeid=2099>.

Hartley, John (1982) *Understanding News*. London: Methuen.

Hiatt, Bethany (2006) 'Examiner Quits Over "Low" OBE Standards', *The West Australian*, 30 March: 1.

Howard, John (2007) Transcript of Kevin Donnelly book launch speech, <http://www.platowa.com/>. (A .pdf file is available at the link, *The Official Word.*)

Hunter, Ian (1994) *Rethinking the School: Subjectivity, Bureaucracy, Criticism*. Sydney: Allen & Unwin.

Indyk, Ivor (1997) 'Kinsella's Hallmarks', *Australian Book Review*, July 1997: <http://home.vicnet.net.au/~abr/July97/indyk.html>.

Kant, Immanuel (1970) 'An Answer to the Question: What is Enlightenment?', trans. Hugh Barr Nisbet, in *Kant's Political Writings*, ed. Hans Siegbert Reiss. Cambridge: Cambridge University Press, 54–60.

Kant, Immanuel (1952) *The Critique of Judgement*, trans. James Creed Meredith. Oxford: Oxford University Press.

Kinsella, John (2008) 'Forest Encomia of the South-West' in *Shades of the Sublime & Beautiful*. Fremantle: Fremantle Press, 105–11.

Kinsella, John (2006) *Fast, Loose Beginnings: A Memoir of Intoxications*, Carlton: Melbourne University Press.

Kitching, Gavin (2008) *The Trouble with Theory: The Educational Costs of Postmodernism*. Sydney: Allen & Unwin.

Leavis, Frank Raymond (1974) 'The Priestly Travesty' in *F.R. Leavis Letters in Criticism*, ed. John Tasker. London: Chatto and Windus.

Leavis, Frank Raymond (1972) *New Bearings in English Poetry: A Study of the Contemporary Situation*. Harmondsworth: Penguin.

Lévi-Strauss, Claude (1966) *The Savage Mind*, trans. John Weightman and Doreen Weightman. Chicago: University of Chicago Press.

Lucy, Niall (2006) 'The New Journalism: A Report on Knowledge' in *Technicity*, eds Louis Armand and Arthur Bradley. Prague: Litteraria Pragensia, 281–316.

Lucy, Niall (2004) *A Derrida Dictionary*. Oxford: Blackwell.

Lucy, Niall (2002) 'Structuralism and the Structuralist Controversy' in *The Edinburgh Encyclopedia of Modern Criticism and Theory*, ed. Julian Wolfreys. Edinburgh: Edinburgh University Press, 743–50.

Lucy, Niall (2001) *Beyond Semiotics: Text, Culture and Technology*. London: Continuum.

Lucy, Niall (1997) *Postmodern Literary Theory: An Introduction*. Oxford: Blackwell.

Lucy, Niall (1995) *Debating Derrida*. Carlton: Melbourne University Press.

Lucy, Niall and Con Coroneos (1990) 'Any Questions? The 1985 TAE English Literature Paper Revisited', *Southern Review* 23: 1, 48–57.

Lucy, Niall and Steve Mickler (2009) 'The Postmodern Left', *Cultural Studies Review*, 15: 1, 188–96.

Lucy, Niall and Steve Mickler (2006) *The War on Democracy: Conservative Opinion in the Australian Press*. Nedlands: University of Western Australia Press.

Lyotard, Jean-François (1984) *The Postmodern Condition: A Report on Knowledge* (*Theory and History of Literature*, Vol. 10), trans. Geoffrey Bennington and Brian Massumi. Minneapolis: University of Minnesota Press.

Lyotard, Jean-François and Jean-Loup Thébaud (1985) *Just Gaming* (*Theory and History of Literature*, Vol. 20), trans. Wlad Godzich. Minneapolis: University of Minnesota Press.

Macintyre, Stuart (2007) 'Polemic Fails Its Own Test', *The Australian Literary Review*, March: <http://www.theaustralian.news.com.au/story/0,20867,21275638-25132,00.html>.

McIntyre, Margaret (2001) 'English: The State of the Art', special issue of *Interpretations: Journal of the English Teachers Association of Western Australia*, March.

Norrie, Justin (2005) 'Deconstructing Buffy Leaves Nelson Clueless', *The Sydney Morning Herald*, 6 August: <http://www.smh.com.au/news/national/deconstructing-buffy-leaves-nelson-clueless/2005/08/05/1123125908862.html>.

Patai, Daphne and Wilfrido Corral, eds (2005) *Theory's Empire*. New York: Columbia University Press.

Patton, Paul and Terry Smith, eds (2001) *Jacques Derrida: Deconstruction Engaged, The Sydney Seminars*. Illinois: University of Illinois Press.

Plato (1952) *Phaedrus*, trans. R. Hackford. Cambridge: Cambridge University Press.

Rudd, Kevin (2006) 'Faith in Politics', *The Monthly*, October: <http://www.themonthly.com.au/excerpts/issue17_excerpt_001.html>.

Savige, Jaya (2006) '[Review of] *Fast, Loose Beginnings: A Memoir of Intoxications*', *The Sydney Morning Herald*, 21 August: <http://www.smh.com.au/news/book-reviews/fast-loose-beginnings-a-memoir-of-intoxications/2006/08/21/1156012451866.html>.

Slattery, Luke (2007a) 'Supposed Defenders of Democracy Err in Choice of Foes', *The Australian*, 15 March: <http://www.theaustralian.news.com.au/story/0,20867,21382792-7583,00.html>.

Slattery, Luke (2007b) 'A Travesty of Logic', *On Line Opinion*, 9 March: <http://www.onlineopinion.com.au/view.asp?article=5597>.

Slattery, Luke (2005a) 'Put Literacy Before "Radical" Vanity', *The Australian*, 30 July: <http://www.theaustralian.news.com.au/story/0,20867,16089271-7583,00.html>.

Slattery, Luke (2005b) '"Mumbo Jumbo" Teaching to End', *The Australian*, 4 August: <http://www.theaustralian.news.com.au/story/0,20867,16145987-2702,00.html>.

Stiegler, Bernard (2002) 'The Discrete Image' in Jacques Derrida and Bernard Stiegler, *Echographies of Television: Filmed Interviews*, trans. Jennifer Bajorek. Cambridge: Polity.

Swift, Jonathan (1729) *A Modest Proposal*: <http://art-bin.com/art/omodest.html>.

Turner, Graeme (2007) 'Cultural Literacies, Critical Literacies, and the English School Curriculum in Australia', *International Journal of Cultural Studies*, 10, 1: 105–14.

Wark, McKenzie (2000) 'Generator: Thinking Through John Kinsella's Genre' in *Fairly Obsessive: Essays on the Works of John Kinsella*, eds Rod Mengham and Glen Phillips. Fremantle: Fremantle Arts Centre Press, 250–73.

Welch, Dylan and AAP (2006) 'PM Blasts "Rubbish" Books in Schools', *The Sydney Morning Herald*, 20 April: <http://www.smh.com.au/news/national/pm-blasts-rubbish-books-in-schools/2006/04/20/1145344197107.html>.

Windschuttle, Keith (2007) 'The Struggle for Australian Values in an Age of Deceit', *Quadrant*, January: <http://www.quadrant.org.au/php/article_view.php?article_id=2390>.

Wittgenstein, Ludwig (1953) *Philosophical Investigations*, trans. Gertrude Elizabeth Margaret Anscombe, eds G.E.M Anscombe and Georg Henrik von Wright. Oxford: Blackwell.

INDEX

ABOUT THE AUTHOR

Niall Lucy is a Research Fellow in the Humanities at Curtin University. His books include *Postmodern Literary Theory: An Introduction*, *A Derrida Dictionary* and (with Steve Mickler) *The War on Democracy: Conservative Opinion in the Australian Press*. His previous books for Fremantle Press (co-edited with Chris Coughran) are *Vagabond Holes: David McComb and The Triffids* and *Beautiful Waste: Poems by David McComb*. His book with John Kinsella, *The Ballad of Moondyne Joe*, is forthcoming from Fremantle Press in 2011.

Contact the author at *www.facebook.com/niall.lucy*

Published 2010
FREMANTLE PRESS
25 Quarry Street, Fremantle
(PO Box 158, North Fremantle, 6159)
Western Australia
www.fremantlepress.com.au

Copyright © Niall Lucy, 2010.

This book is copyright. Apart from any fair dealing for the purposes of private study, research, criticism or review, as permitted under the Copyright Act, no part may be reproduced by any process without written permission. Enquiries should be made to the publisher.

Consultant editor Georgia Richter
Cover design Ally Crimp
Cover photograph James Wills
Typeset in Mercury Text G2 9.5/14 pt
and printed on 67 gsm Alternative Book

A catalogue record for this book is available from the National Library of Australia

ISBN 9781921361845 (paperback)

Fremantle Press is supported by the Western Australian State Government through the Department of Cultural Industries, Tourism and Sport.

Fremantle Press respectfully acknowledges the Whadjuk people of the Noongar nation as the Traditional Owners and Custodians of the land where we work in Walyalup.